FIRST
FIELD
GUIDE

ROCKS
AND
MINERALS

NATIONAL AUDUBON SOCIETY

FIRST FIELD GUIDE

ROCKS AND MINERALS

Written by

Edward Ricciuti
Margaret W. Carruthers

Scholastic Inc.

New York   Toronto   London   Auckland   Sydney

The National Audubon Society, established in 1905, has 550,000 members and more than 500 chapters nationwide. Its mission is to conserve and restore natural ecosystems, focusing on birds and other wildlife, and these guides are part of that mission. Celebrating the beauty and wonders of nature, Audubon looks toward its second century of educating people of all ages.

For information about Audubon membership, contact:

National Audubon Society

700 Broadway

New York, NY 10003-9562

212-979-3000   800-274-4201

http://www.audubon.org

Copyright © 1998 by Chanticleer Press, Inc.
All rights reserved. Published by Scholastic Inc.
SCHOLASTIC and associated logos are trademarks and/or registered trademarks of Scholastic Inc.

LIBRARY OF CONGRESS CATALOGING-IN-PUBLICATION DATA
Ricciuti, Edward R.
National Audubon Society first field guide to rocks and minerals/Edward Ricciuti, Margaret W. Carruthers.
p. cm.
Includes index.
Summary: Detailed full-color spreads help beginning naturalists observe and understand over 150 types of rocks and minerals.
ISBN 0-590-05484-8   ISBN 0-590-05463-5
1. Rocks—Collection and preservation—Juvenile literature. 2. Minerals—Collection and preservation—Juvenile literature. [1. Rocks—Collection and preservation. 2. Minerals—Collection and preservation.] I. National Audubon Society.
II. Title.
QE432.2.R327   1998
552.—dc21   97-17991   CIP   AC

ISBN 0-590-05463-5 (HC)
ISBN 0-590-05484-8 (PB)

10 9 8 7 6 5 4 3 2 1   8   9/9   0/0   01   02

Printed in Hong Kong
First printing, April 1998

Contents

The world of rocks and minerals

How to look at rocks and minerals

Field guide

Reference

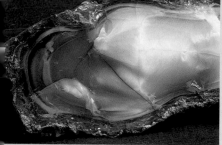
Opal

About this book

Whether you are looking at rocks in your own backyard, strolling along a beach, or trekking through the Grand Canyon, this book will help you see rocks and minerals the way a geologist does. The book is divided into four parts:

Part 1: The world of rocks and minerals introduces you to the basics of geology and mineralogy, the fascinating work of scientists specializing in these fields, and the hobby of rock hunting and collecting.

Part 2: How to look at rocks and minerals gives you the information you need to begin identifying rocks and minerals in the field; provides facts about the specimens you are most likely to see; and explains how rocks and minerals are classified and what they can tell you about the earth.

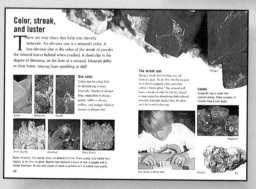

Part 3: The field guide includes detailed descriptions and dramatic photographs of 50 important rocks and minerals. This section also provides shorter descriptions and photographs of over 120 other interesting specimens.

Part 4: The reference section at the back of the book includes a helpful glossary of technical terms used by geologists and naturalists; lists of useful books, organizations, videotapes, software, and Web sites; and an index of rocks and minerals covered in the field guide.

What is a geologist?

If you have an inquiring mind and sharp eyes, you have what it takes to be a geologist. A geologist is a scientist who studies rocks and minerals. Professional geologists use tools such as picks, knives, and goggles, but beginning rock hounds need no more than a notebook and a pencil to get started. Drawing pictures and writing down your observations will help you identify and learn about the interesting rocks and minerals you find.

Florence Bascom (1862–1945) studied geology in college. After graduating, she tried to continue her studies at Johns Hopkins University. The school, however, did not yet admit women. But she did not give up, and in 1893, Florence Bascom became the first woman in the United States to receive a doctor's degree in geology.

Raw garnets

Pick up a rock and look at it closely. Is it multicolored or all one color? Feel it with your hand. Is it smooth or rough, hard or soft? Can you crumble it with your fingers or scratch it with your fingernail? Record your observations. You are now on your way toward being a geologist!

A GEOLOGIST'S TOOLS

Pictured above are some of the tools that geologists use when collecting rocks and minerals: sturdy hiking boots, heavy gloves, goggles, a pick, a pocketknife, a magnifying glass, a small paintbrush (for brushing dirt off rocks), and a field guide.

Rules for rock hunting

- Take a partner with you, preferably an adult.
- Do not wander into places that are not familiar to you.
- Stay away from roadcuts (roads that are cut through huge rocks).
- Before visiting a place, make sure that rock collecting is allowed there.
- Always ask a landowner for permission before entering property.
- Respect nature. Do not disturb living things and do not litter.

What is a mineral?

What do gold, diamonds, rock salt, and ice have in common? They are all minerals. Most rocks are made of minerals. Minerals are natural (not human-made) solid substances. Every mineral has a definite chemical composition. And every mineral's atoms are arranged in a specific way, giving it a crystalline structure. Although ice is a mineral, water is not because it is liquid and does not have a crystalline structure. The properties of a particular mineral—its color, hardness, density, crystal form, the way it breaks—all depend on the elements it is made of, and the way that these elements are arranged and bonded together.

Feldspar crystals

SILICATES
are the most abundant minerals. They are formed from atoms of oxygen and silicon. Examples of silicates include feldspar, mica, topaz, and quartz. Silicates make up most of the rock in the earth's crust.

CARBONATES
Calcite is one of the most common minerals, but it is not a silicate. It's a carbonate: it contains carbon and oxygen rather than silicon and oxygen.

Calcite crystals

Sulfur crystals

ELEMENTS

Most minerals are
mixtures of different
chemical substances
called elements.
Some, such as sulfur
and gold, are made up
of just one element. These are
often called "native elements."

Amethyst geode

GEODES

A geode is a rounded mass of rock that has
a cavity lined with crystals or mineral matter.
The geode at left is filled with crystals of the
mineral amethyst (a type of quartz).

A MINERALOID FROM SAP

Amber is hardened, fossilized sap
from prehistoric trees. It is like a
mineral but is technically not one
because it does not have either a
specific chemical composition or
a crystalline structure. Geologists
refer to amber as a "mineraloid."
Small plants and creatures
trapped in the sap have been
preserved for millions of years.

*Prehistoric insect
preserved in amber*

11

What is a rock?

A rock is a mixture of one or more minerals. The earth is made of layers of rock. The outermost layer is the crust. It is solid and covers the planet like a shell. Below the crust is the mantle, made of rock that is hot but not melted. The next layer down is the outer core, which is hot melted rock. The inner core of the Earth is solid. Scientists think the core is made of the metals iron and nickel. Most rocks that we see come from the Earth's crust.

Mineral mixes

Most rocks are mixtures of many different minerals. Some are made of two or three minerals. A few rocks, such as marble and limestone, are made of only one mineral.

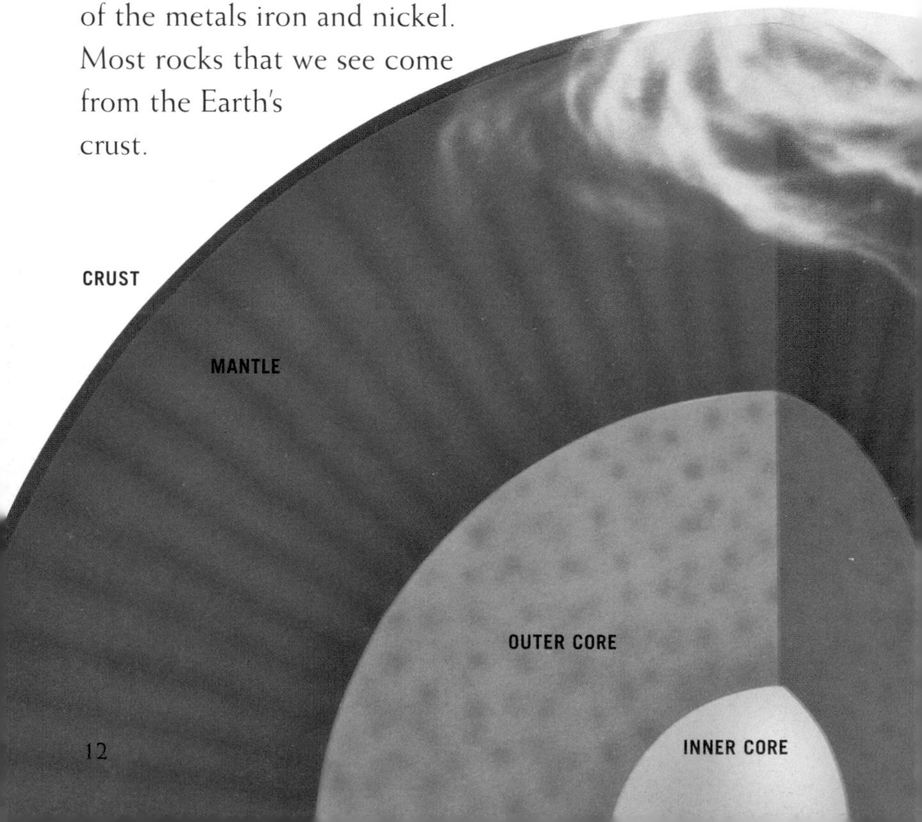

CRUST

MANTLE

OUTER CORE

INNER CORE

Dolomite marble

Pure marble is a rock that contains just one mineral: calcite or dolomite.

Stalactites

ROCKS THAT COME FROM WATER

Stalactites that hang in caves are actually rocks. They are formed by calcite dissolved in water that seeps through from the ground above. As the water meets the air in the cave, the calcite is released, leaving behind a coating in the form of rock. It can take thousands of years for a stalactite to reach a length of just a few feet.

Coal

ROCKS THAT BURN

Coal is a rock made from the remains of plants in ancient forests. Over millions of years the dead plants became buried under layers of sand, mud, and more dead plants. The layers piled up, squeezing the plants below until they hardened into solid coal.

A MASS OF LAVA

Shiprock, in New Mexico, is a mass of lava 1,400 feet high. It built up inside the cone of a volcano that later eroded away, leaving this huge basalt rock formation exposed.

Shiprock, New Mexico

The three classes of rock

Most rocks come from other rocks. Forces on and below the earth's surface continually make new rocks out of old ones. Wind, flowing water, and ice break down rocks into bits and pieces. Heat and pressure deep in the earth can change one type of rock into another. There are three basic types, or classes, of rock—igneous, sedimentary, and metamorphic.

Igneous rock

Igneous rock forms when hot, melted rock deep in the earth cools and becomes solid. Melted, or molten rock beneath the earth's surface is called magma. When magma makes its way to the surface, as it does when a volcano erupts, it is called lava. Magma that cools slowly inside the earth forms one type of igneous rock; lava that cools quickly above the earth's surface forms another type.

Like most igneous rock, granite is very hard. It forms when magma cools slowly deep in the crust of the earth.

Granite: igneous rock

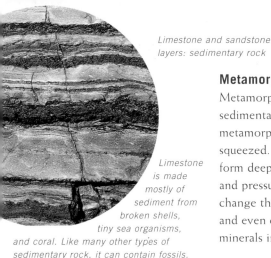

*Limestone and sandstone
layers: sedimentary rock*

Metamorphic rock

Metamorphic rock forms when
sedimentary, igneous, or other
metamorphic rock is heated or
squeezed. Most metamorphic rocks
form deep inside the earth where heat
and pressure are intense enough to
change the shape of mineral crystals
and even change one group of
minerals into another.

*Limestone
is made
mostly of
sediment from
broken shells,
tiny sea organisms,
and coral. Like many other types of
sedimentary rock, it can contain fossils.*

Sedimentary rock

Fragments of shells, stones, or
plants that accumulate on the
bottom of lakes, rivers, and seas
are called sediment. Over time,
the weight of the upper layers
of sediment squeezes those
below until the layers
stick together, forming
solid rock.

Metamorphic rock

*The above photograph
shows sedimentary rock
that has been changed by
tremendous heat and
pressure into metamorphic
rock.*

Volcanoes

Volcanoes are mountains built of layers of lava, which cool and harden to become rock. Some volcanoes, like Hawaii, are formed of fluid (watery) lava that erupts quietly, forming low-lying shield volcanoes. Other magmas are thicker and stickier and have gases dissolved within them. As the magma moves toward the Earth's surface, the pressure drops, allowing the gases to escape. This results in violent eruptions of ash, bombs, and lava flows that form steep-sided volcanoes like Mount St. Helens.

CONES OF CINDERS

Cinder cones are piles of lava ashes and cinders that were blasted out of the earth. They are often found on the slopes of volcanoes.

MAKING MOUNTAINS

Lava is melted rock that flows out of a volcano. As the lava cools, it becomes solid rock again. Layers of cooled lava build up, eventually forming mountains.

Kilauea, Hawaii

EXPLODING MOUNTAIN

In 1980 Mount Saint Helens, in Washington state, exploded after lying quiet for over 100 years. The top was blown off, leaving the mountain more than 1,000 feet shorter. Volcanic ash spewed into the atmosphere and was spread around the world.

Mount Saint Helens

BIG HOLES

Huge craters form when a volcano explodes or collapses. Crater Lake in Oregon fills the hole left by a volcano that caved in after it erupted. The lake is almost 2,000 feet deep.

Crater Lake, Oregon

What is igneous rock?

Deep in the earth's crust, there are places where the rock has melted into magma: a mixture of crystals and liquid rock. Sometimes magma erupts out of the earth through a volcano; then it is called lava. When the lava cools and solidifies on the earth's surface, it forms what is known as volcanic igneous rock. If the magma cools and hardens under the ground, it is called plutonic igneous rock.

Granite

Obsidian

PLUTONIC

Granite, a plutonic rock, forms as magma cools and hardens slowly under the ground. Plutonic rocks generally contain large crystals and are coarse-grained. These rocks are named after Pluto, the Roman god of the underworld.

VOLCANIC

Obsidian, a volcanic rock, cools and hardens so fast that crystals do not have time to form.

LARGE AND SMALL CRYSTALS

Porphyry is an igneous rock that has both large grains like plutonic rock and tiny grains like volcanic rock. The large grains crystallize underground. They are brought to the surface with lava, which cools quickly, causing small crystals to form around larger ones.

Porphyry

Pumice is much lighter than it appears.

Devil's Tower

Devil's Tower in Wyoming is made of an igneous rock called phonolite porphyry. Sixty million years ago, magma forced its way up inside a volcano toward the Earth's surface, but did not erupt out the top. It cooled and hardened under the ground. As softer rocks around it were worn away, the tower of porphyry was exposed.

Devil's Tower, Wyoming

SMALL CRYSTALS

Basalt is a volcanic rock that cools quickly on the surface, allowing only tiny crystals to form.

Basalt

The man in the photo below is holding chunks of pumice, the only rock light enough to float. It's filled with holes formed by gases that escaped as the lava cooled.

How to identify igneous rock

I t is relatively easy to tell the difference between the two main types of igneous rocks. In plutonic rocks, the crystal grains are fairly large and visible. Volcanic rocks usually have small (sometimes microscopic) crystals. A few volcanic rocks lack crystals altogether and are smooth and glassy. If you find a fossil in a rock, you can be almost certain it isn't an igneous rock at all.

Granite contains shiny mineral grains.

ROCKS THAT TWINKLE

Among the most common and easy-to-spot minerals in igneous rocks are feldspars and quartz. They are the light-colored (usually gray, cream, white, or pink) shiny grains in many coarse-grained igneous rocks, such as granite. When these rocks are rotated in sunlight, they reflect light as if they were covered with tiny mirrors.

CHECK THE SURFACE

A rock's surface texture can be a clue to its identity. Volcanic obsidian has a sleek, glossy surface with no crystals. Gabbro, on the other hand, is a plutonic rock with a rough surface and very visible crystals.

Gabbro

Obsidian

Dacite is a medium-colored rock.

In dark-colored igneous rocks such as basalt, at least two-thirds of the minerals are dark.

Basalt veins in granite

LIGHT AND DARK

Igneous rocks have three shades of color—light, medium, and dark—determined by the amounts of light and dark minerals in the rock. The minerals in a medium-colored rock like dacite are about half light and half dark.

In light-colored rocks such as granite, no more than one-third of the minerals are dark.

FINE-, MEDIUM-, OR COARSE-GRAINED?

Can you tell which of the two igneous rocks below—rhyolite and syenite—is plutonic and which is volcanic? One clue is the size of the crystal grains in the rock. Syenite, which is plutonic, is medium- to coarse-grained. Rhyolite, which is volcanic, is fine-grained. You would need a microscope to see most of the crystals in rhyolite.

Rhyolite

Syenite

What is sedimentary rock?

The breakdown of rock is called erosion. Wind and water cause erosion, breaking off fragments of rock and carrying them from one place to another. These fragments can settle almost anywhere, on land or at the bottom of the sea. Gradually, the fragments—along with sand, pebbles, shells, and plant matter—accumulate in layers of what is called sediment. Over a long period of time the sediment hardens into rock. Most of the rock exposed on the earth's surface is sedimentary.

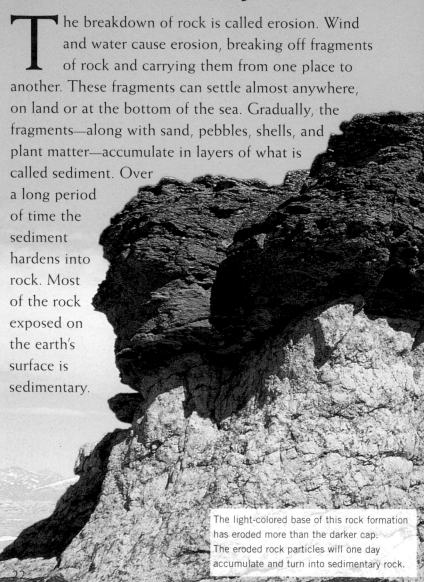

The light-colored base of this rock formation has eroded more than the darker cap. The eroded rock particles will one day accumulate and turn into sedimentary rock.

BIG PARTICLES AND LITTLE ONES

The particles that stick together to make sedimentary rocks come in many different sizes. Tiny particles, like sand grains, form rocks with a fine to medium grain, such as sandstone. Larger, more rounded pieces of rock, such as pebbles, form rocks known as conglomerates.

STONES FROM ANIMALS

Limestone often forms on the sea floor from the accumulated shells and skeletons of sea creatures.

PANCAKES

Layers of sediment stack up like pancakes as they turn into rock. Although laid down flat, the layers are often slanted because of movements of the earth's crust.

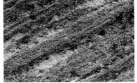

Sandstone

Conglomerate

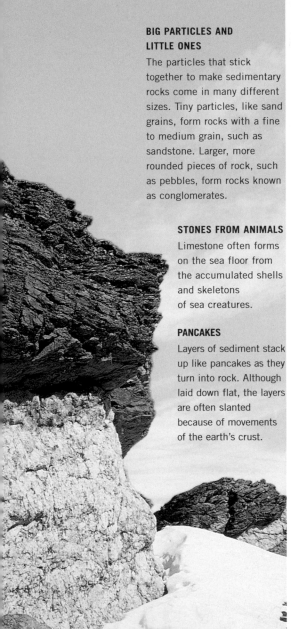

Limestone

Roadcut showing slanted layers of sedimentary rock

23

How to identify sedimentary rock

Shale with fossilized fish

Formations of sedimentary rock are layered, usually in different colors. They can often be seen in roadcuts along highways or in river gorges. Sometimes you can see layers even in small samples of sedimentary rock. Another clue to identifying sedimentary rocks is the presence of fossils—the remains, imprints, and traces of ancient animals and plants. Many sedimentary rocks have fossils, but very few metamorphic rocks or igneous rocks do.

FILLED WITH FOSSILS
Because they contain fossils of plants and animals that lived millions of years ago, sedimentary rocks can help scientists learn about the history of life on Earth.

SOFT AS A ROCK
Generally, sedimentary rocks are soft. Some, like clay, are so soft you can break them with your hands. If you can crumble, split or break a rock with your hands, it is probably sedimentary.

Sandstone with shell fossils

Clay

BIG STUFF, LITTLE STUFF
Rocks containing big fragments of shells and pebbles are sedimentary. But some sedimentary rocks, such as mudstone and shale, have very small mineral grains and therefore are very smooth.

24

Mudstone

MUDSTONE

One common sedimentary rocks is mudstone, whose layers are made up of very tiny particles. Mudstone is so soft it sometimes breaks up in water.

ROCKS WITH RIPPLES

Sedimentary rocks often contain ripple-like markings. They were made in loose sediment (like sand) by moving water. When the sediments solidified into rock, the marks remained.

25

What is metamorphic rock?

Just as cookie dough changes as it is baked, rock changes as it is heated, squeezed, or both. Rock deep within the earth is subjected to intense heat and pressure. In time, these forces change sedimentary or igneous rock into another type of rock: a metamorphic rock. If this new rock is heated or squeezed even more, it can change into another type of metamorphic rock.

When a rock metamorphoses, or changes, its crystals change. A metamorphic rock may look different from its parent rock. Compare each rock on these pages with the rock it becomes.

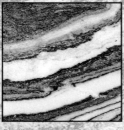

Phyllite

When slate is heated and squeezed, it turns into phyllite. You can see more mica crystals shining in phyllite than in slate.

Shale

Shale, a sedimentary rock, is soft and can contain fossils. Under heat and pressure shale becomes slate—a metamorphic rock. The fossils are destroyed in the process.

Slate

Slate is harder than shale. It lies in flat, flaky layers, which are easily split. Sheets of slate are used for walkways, blackboards, and roofs.

Gneiss

Schist that is subjected to intense heat and pressure can turn into gneiss (pronounced *NICE*). Scientists believe that much of the rock deep within the continental earth is gneiss.

Schist

When phyllite undergoes heat and pressure, it changes into schist. Schist is harder than slate. It is coarse-grained, with large visible crystals.

Marble is a metamorphic rock formed from limestone, a sedimentary rock. Since ancient times marble has been used for sculptures and buildings. It is easy to cut and polish and comes in many different textures and colors. The Lincoln Memorial in Washington, D.C. is made of marble.

Lincoln Memorial, Washington, D.C.

How to identify metamorphic rock

Most metamorphic rock is formed by heat and pressure. It has crystals that are parallel to one another, point in the same direction, and are arranged in layers or bands. Some metamorphic rock, however, is formed by heat alone. The crystals in this type of metamorphic rock lie at many different angles to one another and may not be arranged in layers or bands.

Schist

Gneiss

Which is which?

Heat and pressure gradually turn schist into gneiss. However, there is no clear way to determine at which point schist has become gneiss. They contain similar minerals, arranged in layers in both rocks, and can be very difficult to distinguish because they grade into each other.

Sure bet

Several minerals can form only in metamorphic rock. If you find one of them in a rock, you can bet it is metamorphic, or sedimentary rock that came from eroded metamorphic rock. These minerals include:

Andalusite

Actinolite

Kyanite

Graphite

Staurolite

Talc

Red slate

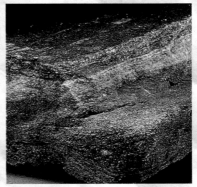
Amphibolite

Go with the grain—sometimes

Grain size can be a clue to the identity of a metamorphic rock. Slate is smooth and has a very fine grain. The grains are so small they can't be seen without a microscope. Amphibolite comes in many versions, varying from fine- to coarse-grained. Some types of amphibolite have crystals arranged in a mosaic pattern, others have crystals arranged in layers.

29

Color, streak, and luster

There are may clues that help you identify minerals. An obvious one is a mineral's color. A less obvious clue is the color of the streak of powder the mineral leaves behind when crushed. A third clue is the degree of shininess, or the luster of a mineral. Minerals differ in their luster, varying from sparkling to dull.

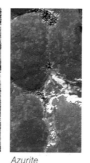

One color

Color can be a big help in identifying certain minerals: Azurite is always blue, malachite is always green, sulfur is always yellow, and realgar (shown above) is always red.

Sulfur   *Malachite*   *Azurite*

Clear Quartz   *Amethyst*   *Rose Quartz*

Some minerals, like quartz, occur in different colors. Pure quartz, also called rock crystal, is as clear as glass. Quartz that contains a trace of iron is purple and is called amethyst. Quartz with traces of rutile is pinkish and is called rose quartz.

The streak test

Using a streak test can help you tell minerals apart. To do this, rub the mineral on a tile of unglazed white porcelain, called a "streak plate." The mineral will leave a streak of color on the tile. Streak is most useful for identifying dark-colored minerals. Minerals harder than the plate can't be tested in this way.

Realgar

Luster

Aragonite has a luster that appears glassy. Many samples of howlite have a dull luster.

Aragonite

Boy doing a streak test

Howlite

31

Crystal shapes

When a mineral has a lot of room and time to grow, it can form beautiful geometric forms known as crystals. There are many crystal forms, and a single mineral may have several shapes. More than 300 forms of calcite have been found. The crystal forms that a particular mineral can take depend on how its atoms are arranged. The shapes that you see depend on this and on the environment that the mineral grew in.

Beryl (aquamarine) crystals are six-sided columns (hexagons).

Fluorite crystals form eight-sided blocks (octahedrons).

Copper crystals often branch out as they grow.

Pyrite crystals have faces marked with parallel grooves called striations.

Crystals of orthoclase tend to be stubby.

Wulfenite crystals may be flattened, like plates.

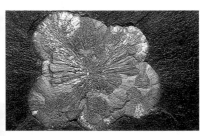

Marcasite crystals may radiate outward.

Crystals of natrolite are usually long and slender.

CLEAVAGE AND FRACTURE

The way a mineral breaks also provides valuable information about its identity. Crystals of some minerals break along planes called cleavages. Some minerals have several cleavages; some have none. Mica (below) is said to have one perfect cleavage, making it very easy to peel crystals apart. An uneven break is called a fracture. Quartz is said to have conchoidal fracture, which means that it breaks along smooth, curved surfaces.

Mica crystals peel apart.

Quartz has conchoidal fracture.

Hardness and weight

The hardness of a mineral is yet another clue to its identity. Almost 200 years ago, a scientist named Friedrich Mohs devised a scale (called the Mohs' Hardness scale) by which the hardness of minerals could be ranked from 1 to 10. At the high end of the scale (10) he placed diamond, the hardest mineral. At the low end of the scale (1) he put talc, the softest mineral. The field guide section of this book lists the Mohs rating of each mineral, next to the letter *H* for "hardness."

5. Apatite

3. Calcite

4. Fluorite

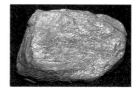

1. Talc

2. Gypsum

The scratch test

Scratch minerals against each other to test their hardness. Harder minerals (those that have a higher number on the Mohs' scale) scratch softer ones. A diamond will scratch all other minerals, whereas talc can't scratch any other.

9. Corundum   **10. Diamond**

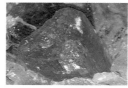

7. Quartz   **8. Topaz**

6. Orthoclase

SCRATCH TOOLS

You can try the scratch test with everyday items. A fingernail has a hardness of 2½, a penny 3½, glass and a penknife 5½, a steel file 6½.

SPECIFIC GRAVITY

Which would weigh more, a one-inch cube of gold or a one-inch cube of talc? The answer is gold—gold has greater density—or weight for its size—than talc. Scientists call the density of a mineral its specific gravity. Gold has a specific gravity rating of 19, while talc's specific gravity rating is about 2.7. (Water's specific gravity is 1.) In the field guide, we give the specific gravity of each mineral, indicated by the letter *G.*

What is a gemstone?

Deep in the Earth, pressure and heat can change minerals of drab, ordinary rock into very hard crystals of incredible beauty. These crystals are gemstones, such as diamonds, rubies, and emeralds, some of which possess nature's most glorious colors. Once cut and polished, a gemstone becomes a gem or a jewel.

Cut diamond

Diamonds are found in an igneous rock called kimberlite. This rock is named after the South African town of Kimberly, site of a famous diamond mine.

Ruby

Storehouses of gems

Most gems form in igneous and metamorphic rock, but many are found in sediments that erode from them.

Turquoise forms in igneous and sedimentary rocks rich in aluminum. Most turquoise deposits are in deserts.

Turquoise

A touch of color

The mineral corundum is made of aluminum and oxygen atoms. When pure, it is colorless. Add a few atoms of chromium, and corundum takes on a blood-red glow and becomes a ruby.

Gems from the past

For thousands of years, people all around the world have used gems to make jewelry and ornaments. The most precious gems were often owned by people of great power. One of the great gem treasure troves of the past has been discovered in the tombs of Egyptian kings, the pharaohs.

King Tut's gold inner coffin inlaid with lapis

A big difference

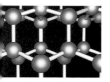

Atoms in a diamond

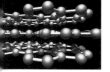

Atoms in graphite

Diamonds and graphite, the "lead" in pencils, contain atoms of only one element, carbon. However, the patterns of their atoms are not the same. And what a difference that makes! Diamonds are clearer than ice, flash like fire, and are the hardest substances on Earth. Graphite is metallic, dark, and soft.

LIGHT SHOW

When light rays enter a cut diamond, the diamond acts as a prism, breaking down the light into the rainbow of colors that make it up. This process is called refraction.

A cut diamond refracting light

Fossils

Rocks are like a book that tells the story of life on Earth. Hidden within many rocks are fossils, the remains of ancient plants and animals. Most fossils are found in sedimentary rock, where they have been preserved, covered in mud, sand, or soil. As the sediments hardened into rock, the fossils were locked in. Fossils are not often found in igneous or metamorphic rock, since the heat and pressure that produce these types of rock destroys fossils.

Ammonite fossil

THE GREAT EXTINCTION

This is a fossil of an ammonite. Ammonites thrived for millions of years. Then, about 65 million years ago, they vanished along with the dinosaurs.

FABULOUS FOSSILS

We have a good idea what dinosaurs such as Tyrannosaurus rex looked like because their bones have been preserved as fossils.

Fossilized skull of Tyrannosaurus Rex

Sometimes, the shells of sea creatures settle to the ocean bottom. The shells dissolve, leaving their imprints in the rock.

FOSSIL FORMATION

Fossils form in many ways, depending on the conditions around them. In Arizona, there are trees that have turned to stone, like the one shown below. The trees died millions of years ago and were buried by sediments. Water carrying dissolved minerals seeped through the ground into the buried logs. The minerals filled the decaying wood, turning it to stone.

Petrified log

FOOTPRINTS FROM THE PAST

Sometimes footprints left in soft soil or mud turn to rock. They are fossils, too. The footprints in the photo to the right were made by ancient humans who walked through wet volcanic ash in Africa about 3.5 million years ago.

How old are rocks and minerals?

The Earth formed about 4.5 billion years ago, but rocks from its original crust have never been found. The oldest known rock formation—a granitic gneiss found in Canada—is more than 3.9 billion years old. Rocks more than 600 million years old are rare. Very old rock exposed by erosion can be seen in the Grand Canyon.

Deposits of Precambrian metamorphic rock found in the Grand Canyon

ROCK CLOCK

By studying the age of rocks, scientists have been able to divide the earth's history into blocks of time called the "Geologic Time Scale." Because rocks older than 600 million years are uncommon, scientists can only estimate the time scale before that date. Below is part of such a time scale:

Cenozoic Era 66 million years ago–Present	Mesozoic Era 245–66 million years ago
Mammals became the dominant life-form on Earth.	Reptiles dominant. Dinosaurs appeared and vanished. First mammals and birds appeared.

Precambrian rocks contain many valuable ores. In the Great Lakes region of the United States and Canada, ores such as iron, copper, nickel, and zinc are mined from these rocks.

Mine in Great Lakes region

This photo shows fossilized algae (single-celled plants) dating from the Precambrian Era. The algae was trapped and fossilized between layers of ancient sedimentary rock.

Fossilized algae

Paleozoic Era
600–245 million years ago

Life diversified. Invertebrates, fishes, amphibians common.

Precambrian Era
4.5 billion–600 million years ago

First fossils, remains of one-celled organisms.

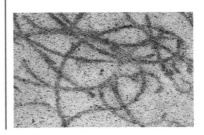

41

Using the field guide

This section highlights 50 common minerals and rocks and briefly covers over 120 more, with photographs and descriptions of each. Generally, specimens on facing pages are similar in some way; sometimes they belong to the same group of minerals or class of rock. A mineral's hardness is indicated next to the letter *H;* its specific gravity is listed next to the letter *G.*

You see double when looking through a calcite crystal.

ICONS

These icons identify minerals and the three classes of rock.

 Minerals

 Igneous rocks

 Sedimentary rocks

 Metamorphic rocks

Cliffs of rhyolite rock

SHAPE ICON
This icon tells you whether the specimen is a mineral or one of the 3 classes of rock.

NAME
The name of the mineral or rock and the class of the rock.

BOX HEADING
The heading alerts you to the other minerals or rocks covered in the box, which are similar in some way to the main one on the page. These box headings include: Other Native Metals, Similar Minerals, Other Salts, Also Found in Pegmatites, Other Forms of Coal, and the like.

GOLD

Gold is one of our most valuable, beautiful, and useful materials. It doesn't tarnish, can be shaped easily, and does not disintegrate over time. It is so long-lasting that gold mined 5,000 years ago is still used today.

PROPERTIES: Very dense and soft, long-lasting; crystals are isometric (blocky), often eight-sided, 12-sided, or cube-shaped, but more common as small flakes or jagged, wiry masses. H=2½–3, G=19.

COLORS: Bright or brassy yellow.

ENVIRONMENT: Gold forms beneath volcanoes in veins in igneous rock and is found with quartz and pyrite. When people pan for gold, they sift through sand from eroded, gold-bearing igneous rock.

SILVER
Native silver is easily shaped, can be hammered into a very thin sheet without breaking, and conducts electricity well. Its silver-white color tarnishes to yellow, brown, or black. The crystals are blocky, usually eight-sided, 12-sided, or shaped like cubes. Silver is found in quartz veins in volcanic rocks and with copper or lead minerals. H=2½–3, G=10.5.

PLATINUM
Platinum is a tin-white or steel-gray native metal. Like silver, it is easily shaped but it does not tarnish. Its crystals are isometric (blocky), usually distorted cubes. It is found in layered igneous rocks with chromite and in sediments with silver. H=4–4½, G=14–19.

45

IDENTIFICATION CAPSULE
The identification capsule covers the details you need to identify a mineral or rock in the field, such as its color, texture, luster, chemical make-up, and how people make use of it.

HARDNESS AND SPECIFIC GRAVITY
The hardness of a mineral (according to the Mohs' scale) is indicated next to the letter H. A mineral's specific gravity (density) is given next to the letter G.

GOLD

Gold is one of our most valuable, beautiful, and useful materials. It doesn't tarnish, can be shaped easily, and does not disintegrate over time. It is so long-lasting that gold mined 5,000 years ago is still used today.

PROPERTIES: Very dense and soft; long-lasting; crystals are isometric (blocky), often eight-sided, 12-sided, or cube-shaped, but more common as small flakes or jagged, wiry masses. H=2½–3, G=19.

COLORS: Bright or brassy yellow.

ENVIRONMENT: Gold forms beneath volcanoes in veins in igneous rock and is found with quartz and pyrite. When people pan for gold, they sift through sand from eroded, gold-bearing igneous rock.

SILVER

Native silver is easily shaped, can be hammered into a very thin sheet without breaking, and conducts electricity well. Its silver-white color tarnishes to yellow, brown, or black. The crystals are blocky, usually eight-sided, 12-sided, or shaped like cubes. Silver is found in quartz veins in volcanic rocks and with copper or lead minerals. H=2½–3. G=10.5.

PLATINUM

Platinum is a tin-white or steel-gray native metal. Like silver, it is easily shaped but it does not tarnish. Its crystals are isometric (blocky), usually distorted cubes. It is found in layered igneous rocks with chromite and in sediments with silver. H=4–4½, G=14–19.

45

Diamonds need very high pressure to form. Most diamonds form more than 75 miles deep into the earth's mantle. Many geologists think that they come to the surface in lava that erupts faster than the speed of sound.

PROPERTIES: Hardest known mineral: can be scratched only by another diamond; forms eight-sided crystals (octahedrons); breaks (cleaves) into perfect eight-sided forms; occurs in nature with a greasy luster. H=10, G=3.5.

COLORS: Clear, yellow, red, blue.

ENVIRONMENT: Diamonds are found in volcanic rocks called kimberlites and in sediments from eroded kimberlites. Diamonds so tiny that they can be seen only under a microscope have been found near craters created by meteorites.

GRAPHITE

Graphite and diamond are the two most common forms of native carbon. But unlike diamond, graphite is very soft, has a metallic luster, a greasy feel, and breaks (cleaves) into flat pieces. Graphite is the "lead" in pencils. It forms when sedimentary rocks that contain carbon-rich minerals or organic materials are metamorphosed. If graphite is buried deep enough or squeezed hard enough by surrounding rocks, it can turn into diamond. H=1–2, G=2.2.

HERKIMER DIAMOND

Herkimer diamonds, although they look like diamonds, are actually quartz crystals. Unlike real diamonds, they can be scratched by harder minerals, such as corundum. H=7, G=2.6.

47

COPPER

Like gold and silver, copper occurs in pure form and can easily be extracted from rocks. Because of this, people were able to use copper for such things as tools and jewelry as far back as 15,000 years ago. Copper is now also used in electronic equipment.

PROPERTIES: Soft, easily shaped, can be hammered thin without breaking; often found as a mass of irregular, treelike shapes, but also forms blocky or cube-shaped crystals. $H=2\frac{1}{2}-3$, $G=9$.

COLORS: Brownish orange; tarnishes to green.

ENVIRONMENT: Native copper has been found in small quantities in sandstones and limestones, but is more common in small holes in basalts. Large deposits occur in northern Michigan.

AZURITE   MALACHITE

Azurite is dark blue; malachite is green. Both are easily cut and polished and are used as gemstones. They can be found with native copper and other copper minerals. Both form when carbonated water (water that has flowed through limestone and absorbed carbon dioxide from it) interacts with other copper minerals or when a copper solution interacts with limestone. Azurite: $H=3\frac{1}{2}-4$, $G=3.8$. Malachite: $H=3\frac{1}{2}-4$, $G=4$.

BORNITE

Bornite is also known as peacock ore because it tarnishes to iridescent colors. It is a minor ore of copper and can be found in veins with such minerals as pyrite and chalcopyrite. $H=3$, $G=5$.

49

PYRITE

Pyrite is also known as fool's gold because people are often "fooled" into thinking they have discovered the real thing. Finding pyrite can still be worthwhile, though, because it often indicates the presence of such important metals as copper, gold, and silver. Pyrite is the most common sulfide mineral.

PROPERTIES: Harder and more brittle than gold but not as dense; forms cube-shaped crystals, often with parallel grooves (striations). H=6–6½, G=5.

COLORS: Brassy or gold.

ENVIRONMENT: Pyrite can be found in many kinds of igneous, sedimentary, and metamorphic rocks, including shale, slate, and quartz veins. Clamshells buried in sulfur-rich mud can become completely covered with pyrite.

MARCASITE
Marcasite has the same chemical make-up as pyrite, but forms crystals that are rectangular rather than cube-shaped. H=6–6½, G=4.9.

CHALCOPYRITE
This is the most important copper ore. It is yellower, softer, and less dense than pyrite. Its crystals have four triangular faces. H=3½–4, G=4.2.

PYRRHOTITE
Pyrrhotite is similar to pyrite, but it is usually magnetic and its crystals are flat, not cube-shaped. Some pyrrhotite contains nickel. H=4, G=4.6.

51

GALENA

Galena is the most important lead mineral. Lead has been used since 4000 B.C. for weapons, ceramics, glassware, and metal alloys. Because lead is highly toxic, its more recent uses in gasoline and paints have been reduced.

PROPERTIES: Dense, very soft; forms cube-shaped or eight-sided crystals (octahedrons); breaks (cleaves) in three directions forming cube shapes. H=2½, G=7.5.

COLORS: Metallic silvery gray; dark gray streak.

ENVIRONMENT: Galena forms when hot water (heated by magma or by warmth from the earth's interior) flows through veins in igneous and sedimentary rock. It is often found with sphalerite, calcite, fluorite, and barite.

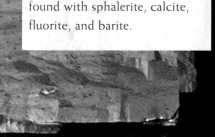

SPHALERITE

Sphalerite is the most important zinc mineral. Zinc is used in electronic equipment, paints, and sunscreens. It is mixed with copper to make bronze. H=3½–4, G=4.

CERUSSITE

Cerussite is a white to dark gray mineral that is found with other lead minerals, commonly in or near limestones. H=3–3½, G=6.6.

WULFENITE

Wulfenite is an orange-red mineral that is sometimes found near galena in lead deposits. H=3, G=6.8.

53

MAGNETITE

Magnetite, as its name suggests, is magnetic. Lodestone is magnetite that is polarized, which means it has north and south ends, allowing it to act as a magnet. When used in compasses, magnetite aligns itself in relation to the earth's North and South Poles. Some small organisms navigate and orient themselves with the help of tiny magnetite crystals that grow within their bodies. Magnetite is mined for iron.

PROPERTIES: Strongly magnetic, forms eight-sided (octahedrons) or 12-sided (dodecahedrons) crystals. H=6, G=5.2.

COLORS: Black; black streak.

ENVIRONMENT: Magnetite occurs with jasper in sedimentary iron formations, with olivine and chromite in igneous and metamorphic rocks, and with other dense and long-lasting minerals in sediments.

CHROMITE

Chromite is mined for chromium, the metal that makes stainless steel hard and resistant to rusting. It forms the same kind of crystals as magnetite, but it is not magnetic. Chromite occurs with olivine in serpentinite rock and in layers with igneous rocks, such as anorthosite and norite. H=5½, G=4.6.

ILMENITE

Ilmenite is found with magnetite in igneous rock and in sediments. Black sand layers at the beach are made of dark, heavy, long-lasting minerals, including ilmenite, rutile, and magnetite. H=5½, G=4.7.

HEMATITE

Hematite often coats igneous and sedimentary rocks with a reddish, rust-like color. The most important iron ore, hematite is used to make steel and other metal mixtures. Its deep color makes it a good pigment in paint.

PROPERTIES: Found in many forms, including six-sided crystals (rhombohedrons), spheres, and earthy masses. H=5½–6½, G=5.3.

COLORS: Red to black; red streak.

ENVIRONMENT: Hematite occurs in many igneous, sedimentary, and metamorphic rocks with other iron minerals, such as magnetite and jasper. The largest deposits of hematite are found in thick sedimentary layers.

LIMONITE

Limonite is the general name given to a mixture of iron oxides, essentially rust, that form when other iron minerals weather, or break down. It gives weathered rocks their typical rusty-brown color. Limonite has a yellow streak. H=5–5½, G=3.6–4.0.

GOETHITE

Goethite is one of the minerals in limonite. It is yellow to red or black with a yellow streak. It is found in many forms, including grapelike masses of crystals and shimmering masses of fibers. H=5–5½, G=4.37.

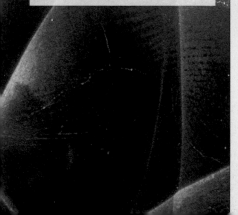

CORUNDUM

Corundum is best known as the gems ruby and sapphire. Ruby, the red variety, gets its color from small amounts of chromium. The blue in sapphire comes from tiny needles of rutile within the mineral. Because it is so hard, corundum is good for grinding and polishing and is used in sandpaper and nail files.

PROPERTIES: Very hard; forms crystals that are six-sided columns; breaks (fractures) into curved shapes. H=9, G=4.

COLORS: White, gray, brown to black, red, blue, yellow, green.

ENVIRONMENT: Corundum forms in igneous rocks called pegmatites that occur with nepheline syenites, and with muscovite, almandine, and quartz in schist and gneiss. Most corundum is mined from sediments.

SPINEL

Because spinel has fewer flaws than ruby, it was often substituted for rubies in the royal crowns of England and Russia. Spinel is softer than corundum and usually forms blocky, eight-sided crystals. H=8, G=3.5–4.1.

SAPPHIRE

All gem-quality corundum that is not ruby is called sapphire. Commonly seen as a blue stone, sapphire can also be pink, green, violet, gray, and yellow. H=9, G =4.

RUTILE

Rutile is red to brown to black, and is found within other minerals, such as rose quartz and sapphire, giving them color. H=6–6½, G=4.2.

59

URANINITE

Uraninite, also called pitchblende, is the most important uranium mineral. It is radioactive and is used to generate nuclear power.

PROPERTIES: Forms sooty masses, eight-sided and cube-shaped crystals; breaks (fractures) into curved shapes. H=5½, G=7.5–9.5.

COLORS: Greenish to black; brownish-black streak.

ENVIRONMENT: Uraninite occurs in granite veins and pegmatites (coarse-grained igneous rocks) and in sedimentary rocks, such as sandstones and shales. Sometimes trees that are buried under layers of rock and sediment become uraninite logs: Over the course of time, water with uranium in it slowly seeps into the trees, eventually replacing the trees' organic (living) matter with uraninite.

AUTUNITE

Autunite is a bright yellow-green mineral that forms tabular crystals. It is often found with uraninite and is also radioactive. H=2–2½, G=3.1.

ZIRCON

Zircon occurs as very small crystals in igneous rocks and sediments. It comes in many colors and is used in jewelry as a less expensive diamond substitute. Many zircons contain a small amount of radioactive uranium. H=7½, G=4.7.

MONAZITE

Monazite is yellow, brown, green, or white and forms in granite pegmatites with quartz and feldspar. It is mined for rare elements, such as thorium. H=5–5½, G=4.6–5.4.

RHODOCHROSITE

Rhodochrosite is an important manganese ore. Manganese is used to purify iron and make steel more resistant. It is also used in batteries and to purify water. The name rhodochrosite comes from the Greek words *rhodon* for "rose" and *chros* for "color."

PROPERTIES: Breaks (cleaves) in three directions; forms six-sided crystal prisms with each face being a rhombus. H=3½–4, G=3.5.

COLORS: Pink, brown, or brownish yellow; white streak.

ENVIRONMENT: In veins with calcite, dolomite, fluorite, and barite, and in metamorphic rocks with rhodonite and garnet.

RHODONITE

Rhodonite looks like rhodochrosite, but it is harder, and breaks (cleaves) in only two directions. It is used as a gemstone and as a decorative stone. H=5½–6, G=3.4–3.7.

PYROLUSITE

Pyrolusite forms on the surface of other manganese minerals and in stagnant lagoons. When it has a treelike or branching shape it can be mistaken for a fossilized plant. H=1–2, G=4.75

MANGANITE

Manganite is steel-gray to black with a dark brown streak and forms crystals shaped like columns. It can be found in veins with barite and calcite. H=4, G=4.3.

63

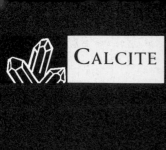

CALCITE

If you look at an object through a clear calcite crystal or fragment, you'll see two objects instead of one. When a ray of light passes through the crystal, it separates into two rays, creating a double image. This type of calcite is known as Iceland spar. Calcite is used in optical instruments, chalk, cement, and lime (for marking lines on playing fields).

PROPERTIES: Occurs in more forms than any other mineral, from uneven-sided, triangular crystals called dog-tooth spar to small round grains called oolites; breaks (cleaves) into perfect six-sided crystals (rhombohedrons); fizzes in vinegar or hydrochloric acid. H=3, G=2.7.

COLORS: Clear, white, pink, red, green, blue; white streak.

ENVIRONMENT: Calcite can be found in many rocks, including limestone, travertine, carbonatites, and marble.

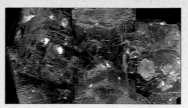

ARAGONITE

Aragonite, like calcite, is a form of calcium carbonate. It is harder and denser than calcite and forms crystals shaped like rectangular columns. Pearls are made of aragonite. H=3½–4, G=2.95.

DOLOMITE

Dolomite is similar to calcite, but it is usually tan and forms distinctive saddle-shaped crystals. It is used to make magnesia for industrial and medicinal purposes. H=3½–4, G=2.8.

SIDERITE

Siderite, yellow to brown, forms in swampy areas. It can be found in layers with other iron minerals (hematite and magnetite). H=4, G=3.9.

65

FLUORITE

Fluorite is the main source of fluorine used for fluoride in toothpaste and drinking water. The word "fluorescent" was coined to describe the way some samples of fluorite glow under ultraviolet light.

PROPERTIES: Forms cube-shaped or eight-sided crystals (octahedrons); breaks (cleaves) into perfect eight-sided shapes. H=4, G=3.18.

COLORS: White, purple, green, pink, yellow.

ENVIRONMENT: Fluorite forms when hot water (heated by magma) or watery molten rock flows through cracks in rocks and leaves minerals behind. Over time, the minerals grow and eventually fill up the cracks. Fluorite is often found with galena, sphalerite, and barite.

BARITE

Barite can be found with fluorite, galena, sphalerite, and in lead-zinc deposits. Because it is dense, barite is used in mud that is put into drill holes to keep oil from erupting. H=3–3½, G=4.5.

APATITE

Apatite occurs as six-sided (hexagonal) crystals in igneous or metamorphic rocks. It is often mistaken for other minerals, such as beryl and tourmaline, because it occurs in many different colors. Apatite is the main mineral found in our teeth and bones. H=5, G=3.2.

67

HALITE

Halite, also called rock salt, is the table salt you sprinkle on french fries and corn on the cob. It also has other uses. Large crystals of halite are spread on roads to melt snow and ice, because saltwater freezes at a lower temperature than pure water. For the same reason, halite is also used in the making of homemade ice cream.

PROPERTIES: Forms cube-shaped crystals; breaks (cleaves) in three directions, all at right angles; salty taste; glows under ultraviolet light (fluorescent). H=2½, G=2.2.

COLORS: Clear, white, or tinted with gray, yellow, red, or blue; white streak.

ENVIRONMENT: Halite is an evaporite—a rock or mineral that forms when water evaporates, leaving behind solids that had been dissolved in the water. It forms in shallow lakes (called playas) in desert areas and can be found both in dried-up lakes and inland seas. Older beds of halite can be found in between layers of sedimentary rock.

SYLVITE

Sylvite is similar to halite in all of its properties and is used as a substitute for table salt. Unlike halite, though, it also forms near volcanoes. H=2, G=1.99.

EPSOMITE

Epsomite, better known as epsom salts, is used for healing (therapeutic) baths. It forms in snowball-like masses or fibers known as hairsalt in caves and mine tunnels. H=2–2½, G=1.7.

69

GYPSUM

Gypsum, a common sulfate mineral, is used to make plaster and cement. Large masses of colorfully banded gypsum, called alabaster, are used to carve sculptures.

PROPERTIES: Breaks (cleaves) in one direction perfectly; breaks into curved shapes (conchoidal fracture). H=2, G=2.32.

COLORS: Clear, white, gray, yellow, red, brown; white streak.

ENVIRONMENT: Like halite and borax, gypsum is an evaporite mineral and forms when water evaporates and leaves behind solids that had been dissolved in it. Gypsum is often found in sedimentary rock between layers of other rock, such as anhydrite and sulfur. Some cave formations, such as stalactites, are made of gypsum rather than calcite.

ANHYDRITE

Anhydrite is a white to bluish to lavender evaporite mineral often found with halite and gypsum. It is harder than gypsum and breaks (cleaves) in three directions, all at right angles. H=3–3½, G=3.

SULFUR

Sulfur can be found in thick sedimentary layers above anhydrite. It also forms in and around hot springs and volcanoes. It is used to make rubber, fertilizers, and weapons. H=1½–2½, G=2.

71

In the 13th century, Marco Polo brought borax from Tibet to Europe. Since then, borax has been an important source of boron, which is used in laundry detergents, insulation, food preservatives, and heat-resistant glass cookware.

PROPERTIES: Forms short, column-shaped crystals; dissolves in water. H=2–2½, G=1.7.

COLORS: Colorless or white to grayish.

ENVIRONMENT: Borax is found in dried-up lakes with other minerals, such as halite and gypsum, that are formed when water evaporates and leaves behind solids that had been dissolved in it.

ULEXITE

Ulexite, a white, satiny mineral, forms in arid regions. It crystallizes as perfect continuous fibers. Also known as television stone, ulexite can transmit light, projecting an image placed under it up to the mineral's surface. H=1–2½, G=1.96.

COLEMANITE

Colemanite is a white to gray or yellowish mineral that occurs as short, column-shaped crystals or masses with other boron minerals, such as borax and ulexite. Like borax and ulexite, it forms in arid regions when water evaporates. H=4–4½, G=2.4.

73

CLEAR QUARTZ

Quartz, a silicon ore, is the most common mineral in the earth's crust. It is used for gemstones and to make glass. Quartz crystals are used in watches and radios because they are piezoelectric: That means they vibrate regularly when an electric current passes through them.

PROPERTIES: Forms six-sided crystal columns with pyramids on the ends; breaks into curved shapes. H=7, G=2.6.

COLORS: Clear, white, purple, pink, blue, yellow.

ENVIRONMENT: Quartz is found in many igneous, sedimentary, and metamorphic rocks, including granite, rhyolite, sandstone, shale, quartzite, schist, and gneiss. Large crystals form near hot springs and in pegmatites.

Quartz can be found in a variety of colors, depending on different impurities or other elements or minerals within the crystals.

AMETHYST

Amethyst is the purple variety of quartz. Its color comes from small amounts of iron within it.

ROSE QUARTZ

Microscopic needles of the mineral rutile cause the pink color of rose quartz.

MILKY QUARTZ

Milky quartz owes its clouded appearance to tiny pockets of liquid or vapor trapped within the mineral.

Opal is not technically a mineral because it does not have a crystalline structure. It is described as being amorphous, which means it does not have a definite form. Opal is composed of tiny balls of silica. The brilliant play of colors in opal gemstones is a result of the way light interacts with the silica balls.

PROPERTIES: Pearly luster; never forms crystals; breaks into curved shapes. H=5–6, G=2.

COLORS: Colorless, white, blue, black, green, orange.

ENVIRONMENT: Opal forms in holes and fractures in rocks, in sediments, and in volcanic rocks. Some petrified wood is composed of opal. (Petrified wood is formed when trees became buried under sediment; over time, minerals seeped in, replacing the trees' cells and resulting in a stone log.)

CHALCEDONY

Chalcedony is quartz that has crystals too tiny to see without a microscope. Like opal, it forms in holes in rocks and can replace organic (living) matter, such as wood and coral. Chalcedony can be found in a variety of colorful forms, including apple-green chrysoprase, red carnelian, banded agate, and heliotrope or bloodstone, which is bright green with red spots.

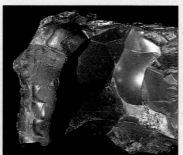

JASPER

Jasper is a red, iron-rich variety of chalcedony. It can be found in sedimentary rocks with other iron minerals, such as hematite and magnetite.

ORTHOCLASE

Orthoclase is a type of potassium feldspar, or K-spar, that can be found in igneous rocks formed below the earth's surface (plutonic rocks). Red and pink granites, which make beautiful building stones, get their color from tiny amounts of iron oxide in orthoclase. K-spar is mined for potassium.

PROPERTIES: Breaks (cleaves) in two directions at right angles to each other. H=6, G=2.6.

COLORS: White, pink, red.

ENVIRONMENT: Orthoclase occurs in many different rock types, including granite, syenite, schist, gneiss, and arkose.

SANIDINE

Sanidine is a colorless or transparent type of potassium feldspar that forms in such volcanic rocks as rhyolite. It often looks like square or rectangular crystals. H=6, G=2.6.

MICROCLINE

Microcline is a type of potassium feldspar that forms in igneous rocks that cool slowly at great depths. Amazonite is a green variety of microcline that gets its color from tiny amounts of lead in the crystal. Microcline can form huge crystals weighing hundreds of tons. H=6, G=2.6.

ALBITE

Albite is the sodium-rich variety of plagioclase feldspars—common rock-forming minerals that are found in igneous and metamorphic rocks. (The other plagioclase feldspars are labradorite, anorthite, oligoclase, andesine, and bytownite.) If you look closely at the face of an albite crystal, you may see parallel grooves called striations. Potassium feldspar, which can look very similar to albite, does not have striations.

PROPERTIES: Breaks (cleaves) into two good directions; intersecting at almost 90 degrees. H=6, G=2.6.

COLORS: White; white streak.

ENVIRONMENT: Albite occurs in igneous rocks, such as granite, rhyolite, syenite, and pegmatite; in metamorphic rocks, such as schist and gneiss; and in sedimentary rocks, such as arkose.

LABRADORITE

Labradorite is a plagioclase found in basalt, gabbro, and anorthosite. It may have a beautiful iridescence, which means the colors can change depending on the direction and angle of the light striking the rock. This feature makes gabbro and anorthosite popular building stones. Labradorite is named for Labrador, Newfoundland, where crystals several feet across have been found. H=6, G=2.7.

ANORTHITE

Anorthite is the darker-colored, calcium-rich variety of plagioclase feldspar. It is found only in certain igneous rocks called anorthosites and in meteorites. H=6, G=2.8.

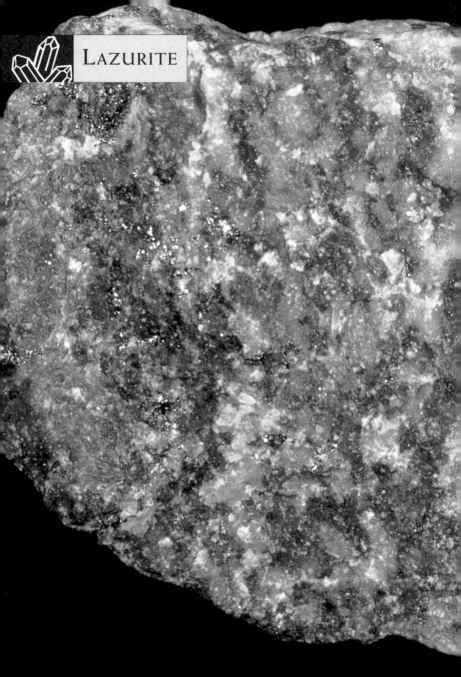

LAZURITE

Lazurite is an azure to greenish-blue member of a group of rock-forming minerals called feldspathoids, which have the same chemical elements but differ in their chemical structure, crystals, and physical characteristics. The gemstone lapis lazuli is lazurite mixed with calcite, pyroxenes, and pyrite.

PROPERTIES: Usually forms masses of tiny crystals; rarely forms visible 12-sided (dodecahedral) crystals. H=5½–6, G=2.4.

COLOR: Azure to greenish blue.

ENVIRONMENT: Lazurite occurs with pyrite in marble and near pegmatites (coarse-grained igneous rocks) in limestone, a sedimentary rock.

SODALITE

Sodalite is a feldspathoid that usually forms in masses. It is usually blue but can also be pale pink, yellow, gray, green, white, or colorless. H=5½–6, G=2.2.

NEPHELINE

Nepheline is a colorless, gray or brownish, greasy-looking mineral that is found with sodalite in phonolites and nepheline syenites. Like other feldspathoids, it is almost never found with quartz. H=5–6, G=2.6.

83

NATROLITE

Natrolite is a type of mineral called a zeolite. Zeolites are used for softening and purifying water. They have a lot of open spaces within their crystals, so when water passes through them, elements in the water, such as calcium, get trapped within the crystals.

PROPERTIES: Forms crystals shaped like long, thin fibers. H=5–5½, G=2.2.

COLORS: White or colorless.

ENVIRONMENT: Zeolites form in such volcanic rocks as tuffs and basalts, in rocks that have been only slightly metamorphosed, and in salty lake deposits. Beautiful crystals of natrolite can be found with other zeolites and with calcite in holes in basalts.

HEULANDITE
Heulandite commonly forms diamond-shaped crystals in holes in basalts. It can be colorless, white, yellow, or red. H=3½–4, G=2.2.

STILBITE
Stilbite forms flat crystals that fan out from a central point. Like other zeolites, it can be white or slightly reddish because of small amounts of iron oxide in it. H=3½–4, G=2.1–2.2.

CHABAZITE
Chabazite can be white, yellow, pink, or red. It forms six-sided crystals (rhombohedrons) similar to calcite, but calcite fizzes in vinegar or acid, and chabazite does not. H=4–5, G=2.1.

BERYL

Beryl is a mineral that occurs in different colors, and each color is a different gemstone. Bright green beryl is emerald; blue-green beryl is aquamarine; yellow to brown beryl is heliodor; and red to pink beryl is morganite. Beryl is also a major source of beryllium, which is mixed with copper to make a hard and elastic alloy used in the aerospace industry. Because it is transparent to X rays, beryllium is used in the windows of X-ray tubes.

PROPERTIES: Forms crystals that are six-sided (hexagonal) columns. H=7½–8, G=2.6–2.9.

COLORS: Green, yellow, pink.

ENVIRONMENT: Beryl can be found in pegmatites (coarse-grained igneous rock) and in schist with quartz, mica, and almandine.

TOURMALINE

There are many types of tourmaline, including rubellite (pink), elbaite (green), and schorl (black). Large crystals have been found in pegmatites; smaller crystals form in mica schists. Unlike beryl crystals, tourmaline crystals have triangular ends. H=7–7½, G=3–3.2.

TOPAZ

Topaz is a hard, glassy, transparent mineral that often forms crystals with rectangular sides. It can be found in granite and rhyolite and in veins in other rocks. Large crystals form in pegmatites. Topaz can be colorless, white, or light yellow, green, red, or blue. H=8, G=3.5.

Augite is the most common pyroxene mineral. Pyroxenes are necessary in order for many rocks to form. When they were named (*pyroxene* comes from Greek words and means "stranger to fire"), it was thought that these minerals never formed in igneous rocks. It was later discovered that most pyroxenes do form in the fiery environment of igneous rocks—but the name stuck.

PROPERTIES: Forms crystals that are short, square columns or have eight sides; breaks (cleaves) in two directions, at almost perfect right angles. H=5–6, G=3.2–3.4.

COLORS: Dark green to black.

ENVIRONMENT: Augite forms in igneous rocks, such as basalt, gabbro, peridotite, pyroxenite, and andesite. It has also been found in moon rocks.

JADEITE
Jadeite is one type of jade. It is found in metamorphic rocks that form when sediments mixed with seawater are pushed beneath the surface by forces deep within the earth. H=6½–7, G=3.3–3.5.

SPODUMENE
Spodumene is a pink to pale green lithium pyroxene. It can form large crystals in pegmatites (coarse-grained igneous rocks) and is often found with such minerals as lepidolite and quartz. H=6½–7, G=3.15–3.2.

89

ACTINOLITE

Actinolite forms strong, long-lasting, and flexible fibers that are resistant to heat and deterioration. Minerals having a fibrous appearance are called asbestiform. Asbestiform actinolite is one of several minerals known commercially as asbestos. Actinolite is in a group of minerals called amphiboles. Actinole's fibers have qualities that make it a good building material. It is not the type of asbestos dangerous to people's health.

PROPERTIES: Often forms a mass of fibers that spread out from a central point. H=5–6, G=3.1–3.3.

COLORS: Dark green.

ENVIRONMENT: Actinolite is found in metamorphic rocks, such as schist, marble, and amphibolite.

NEPHRITE JADE

Nephrite jade is a massive, compact form of actinolite. This type of jade has been used for centuries to make beautiful ornaments. H=5–6, G 3.1– 3.3.

HORNBLENDE

Hornblende is a dark green to black rock-forming mineral common in granite, basalt, diorite, schist, and gneiss. It is also the main mineral in amphibolite. H=5–6, G=3.0–3.4.

91

MUSCOVITE MICA

M uscovite is the clear (transparent) or light-colored mica that makes phyllite and schist sparkle. It is named after the people in Moscow who used it as a substitute for glass. It is now used in paint, wallpaper, and rubber.

PROPERTIES: Breaks (cleaves) into flakes or thin sheets. H=2–2½, G=2.8–2.9.

COLORS: Clear, whitish, gray, or brownish.

ENVIRONMENT: Muscovite is very common in granites and in metamorphic rocks, such as slate, phyllite, and schist.

BIOTITE

Biotite is the dark variety of mica and forms the dark plates in granite and schist. H=2½–3, G=2.8–3.2.

LEPIDOLITE

Lepidolite is a purple lithium mica. It occurs in pegmatites (coarse-grained igneous rocks). Lepidolite is a source of the lithium used in batteries and medicines. H=2½–4, G=2.8–2.9.

MARGARITE

Margarite is brittle rather than flexible and is not as common as other micas. It occurs with corundum and with calcite and quartz in metamorphic rocks such as schist. H=3½–5, G=3.0–3.1.

VERMICULITE

Vermiculite is a clay mineral that gets its name from *vermis*, the Latin word for "worm." When heated, the crystals expand into wormlike shapes. Vermiculite can absorb a lot of water and is useful in soils and mulch.

PROPERTIES: Shiny luster; flaky; looks like biotite but is softer and more flexible. H=1½, G=2.4.

COLORS: White to yellow, and brown.

ENVIRONMENT: Clay minerals are common in fine-grained sedimentary rocks. They form when other minerals weather, or break down. Vermiculite forms when biotite breaks down.

The type of clay mineral that forms depends on the climate and the original mineral. Most clay crystals are so small that it takes special instruments to identify them.

KAOLINITE

Kaolinite is a soft, white, powdery clay mineral that forms from potassium feldspar in warm, humid places with good drainage. It is a type of clay used for ceramics. H=2–2½, G=2.6.

FULLER'S EARTH

Fuller's earth is a soft sediment made primarily of clay minerals. It was first used to remove oil and grease from wool (a process called *fulling*). Today it is used to purify mineral and vegetable oils.

TALC

Talc, one of the softest minerals, is the main ingredient in talcum powder. It is also used for insulation in electrical equipment, and because it has a greasy feel, it is used as a lubricant. Soapstone is a mass of talc that is soft enough to be carved into sculptures with a knife.

PROPERTIES: Usually in a mass or in thin flakes; very soft, slippery feel. H=1, G=2.7–2.8.

COLORS: White to green; white streak.

ENVIRONMENT: Talc can be found in metamorphic rocks, such as talc schist and serpentinite. It forms when other magnesium minerals, such as olivine, break down.

PYROPHYLLITE

Pyrophyllite and talc are often so similar in color, appearance, and feel that it can be almost impossible to tell them apart. Pyrophyllite occurs with kyanite or andalusite in schists. It is used in ceramics, paints, and rubber products. H=1–2, G=2.8.

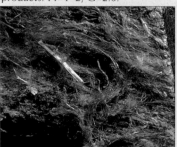

SERPENTINE

There are three forms of serpentine: chrysotile, antigorite, and lizardite. Masses that have an asbestiform appearance (bunches of crystal fibers) can be spun and woven into heat-resistant materials used for insulation. Serpentine forms when olivine breaks down and occurs in metamorphosed basalts and peridotites. H=3–5, G=2.3–2.6.

OLIVINE

Olivine is also known to some as the yellowish to olive-green gemstone peridot.

PROPERTIES: Forms crystals that are usually found as round grains; also as masses; breaks into curved shapes. H=6½–7, G=3.2–4.

COLORS: Yellow-green, green, or brownish green.

ENVIRONMENT: Olivine occurs in igneous rocks, such as basalt, gabbro, and peridotite, and with other minerals such as pyroxene, chromite, magnetite, and plagioclase. Rock composed entirely of olivine is called dunite.

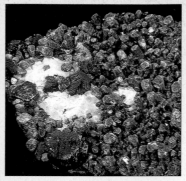

DIOPSIDE

Diopside is a pale green pyroxene similar to augite. It forms stubby crystals with square or rectangular ends. Diopside can be found in metamorphic rocks such as marble, gneiss, and schist, and in igneous rocks such as basalt and peridotite. H=5½ 6½, G=3.3–3.6.

EPIDOTE

Like diopside, epidote is a greenish mineral that forms in metamorphic rock. It is found in seams where igneous rock has come in contact with, and has therefore metamorphosed, limestone. H=6–7, G=3.2–3.5.

99

Staurolite crystals often grow together as two crystals that seem to pass through each other. Geologists call these crystals "penetration twins." Staurolite twins grow at right angles to each other, forming crosses (*stauros* is the Greek word for "cross").

PROPERTIES: Forms irregular prisms. H=7–7½, G=2.2.

COLORS: Yellowish brown, reddish black to brownish black.

ENVIRONMENT: Staurolite is a metamorphic mineral that can be found in schists along with albite, biotite, garnet, tourmaline, and kyanite.

ANDALUSITE

Andalusite is a gray, white, pink, reddish-brown, or olive-green mineral that forms crystals with square-shaped ends. H=7½, G=3.2.

KYANITE

Kyanite forms bladelike crystals that are usually blue, but can also be gray, green, yellow, pink, or black. H=5–7, G=3.55–3.66

SILLIMANITE

Sillimanite forms masses of fibers that spread out in gray or brown crystal columns. H=6–7, G=3.23.

101

Almandine is the most common garnet mineral. Garnets are very hard and most that are mined are used as abrasives for grinding and polishing. Some are beautiful enough for gemstones and are sometimes mistaken for rubies or red spinels. Garnets can be as large as three feet across.

PROPERTIES: Often forms 12-sided crystals (dodecahedrons). H=7, G=4.3.

COLORS: Dark or deep red.

ENVIRONMENT: Almandine is a common mineral found in metamorphic rocks, such as schist and gneiss, that were once sediments. Rounded grains can also be found in beach sands with other hard minerals, such as quartz, magnetite, and ilmenite.

PYROPE

Pyrope is a deep red garnet that is found in eclogites and peridotites—rocks that form very deep within the earth's mantle and crust. H=7, G=3.6.

GROSSULAR

Grossular is a pale green, honey yellow to cinnamon brown garnet found in marble and other calcium-rich metamorphic rocks. H=6½, G=3.6.

SPESSARTINE

Spessartine is a pink garnet. It is the only garnet commonly found in igneous rocks, such as granite and rhyolite. It can also be found in pegmatites along with tourmaline and topaz. H=7, G=4.2.

103

GRANITE

igneous

If we could mix up all the rocks in the earth's continental crust, melt them, and then solidify them, we would get granite. Granite is the most important igneous rock in the crust that makes up the earth's continents. Many igneous rocks are granites, and many sedimentary and metamorphic rocks were once granite. Granite is frequently used as a building stone.

MINERAL COMPOSITION: Quartz, orthoclase and plagioclase feldspars, muscovite.

TEXTURE: Interlocking crystals large enough to see.

COLORS: White, gray, pink, red.

ENVIRONMENT: Granite forms miles below the surface of the earth's crust (and is therefore called a plutonic rock). We can see some of these granite rocks —in such places as Yosemite National Park in California and Acadia National Park in Maine—because the rocks above them have slowly eroded away.

GRANITE PEGMATITE

A pegmatite is an igneous rock, usually granite, with large crystals. Many gem-quality crystals come from pegmatites. They often occur as wall-like sheets that cut across granites and gneisses.

GRANODIORITE

Granodiorite is similar to granite, but is usually white (not pink) because it has less potassium feldspar and more plagioclase feldspar. It may also have biotite and some hornblende.

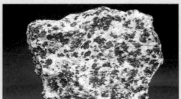

DIORITE

Diorite has almost no quartz and less potassium feldspar and more plagioclase feldspar than granite or granodiorite. It has a salt-and-pepper appearance from black biotite and hornblende.

105

Nepheline syenites are very important because the coarse-grained parts of them (pegmatites) contain rare elements, such as beryllium and uranium, as well as unusual minerals.

MINERAL COMPOSITION:
Nepheline, potassium and plagioclase feldspars, biotite, pyroxene, sodalite, cancrinite.

TEXTURE: Coarse-grained.

COLORS: Light gray with black biotite and pyroxene; bluish if rich in sodalite.

ENVIRONMENT: Nepheline syenites are plutonic rocks that solidified beneath the continental crust while the crust was being torn apart by forces deep within the earth. Nepheline syenites can be found with monzonites, phonolites, and syenites (rocks similar to nepheline syenites, but with quartz instead of nepheline, sodalite, or cancrinite).

MONZONITE

Monzonite is a plutonic rock (solidified beneath the continental crust) similar to syenite but with more plagioclase feldspar and less potassium feldspar. It may have quartz, but if it contains nepheline, sodalite, or cancrinite instead of quartz, it is known as a foid-monzonite. *Foid* is short for "feldspath*oid*."

LARVIKITE

Larvikite is a special type of blue-gray syenite or monzonite containing iridescent feldspar crystals that sparkle with different colors, depending on the direction and angle of the sunlight striking them. Larvikite makes a beautiful building stone.

PYROXENITE

Pyroxenite is a rock composed almost entirely of large crystals of pyroxene minerals, such as augite and bronzite. It solidifies deep in the earth's crust. Some meteorites from Mars are pyroxenites.

PERIDOTITE

Peridotite is an olivine-pyroxene rock (sometimes with garnet) that comes from the earth's mantle. Pieces of peridotite can sometimes be found within basalt. It is coarser grained than basalt because it solidifies more slowly and deeper in the mantle.

Gabbro, with its large crystals of dark-colored pyroxenes (silicate minerals) and iridescent plagioclase feldspar, is a popular building stone.

MINERAL COMPOSITION: Pyroxene, calcium-rich plagioclase feldspar, olivine.

TEXTURE: Medium to coarse-grained interlocking-crystals.

COLORS: Dark gray to greenish or bluish black.

ENVIRONMENT: Gabbro is the same as basalt, but it has larger crystals. Most of it forms deep within the oceanic crust, beneath basalt.

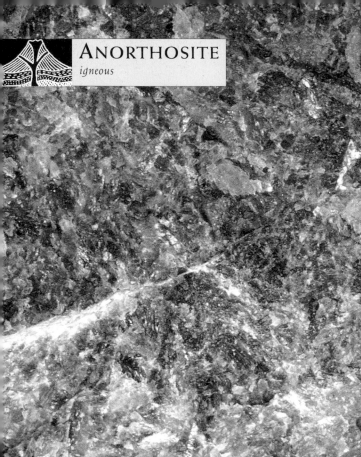

I f you look up at the moon on a clear night, you'll see the moon's light and dark sections. The light-colored sections (the highlands) are made of anorthosite and other plagioclase-rich rocks. Many geologists think the rocks solidified from an ocean of magma that covered the moon some four billion years ago.

MINERAL COMPOSITION: Calcium plagioclase with small amounts of pyroxene, quartz, and orthoclase.

TEXTURE: White, coarse-grained crystals can be interlocking, or look as though they have settled out on top of each other.

COLORS: White to light gray.

ENVIRONMENT: Anorthosites are plutonic igneous rocks that formed deep in the earth's crust. Many occur in layers with other plutonic rocks.

NORITE

Norite contains large crystals of plagioclase and pyroxene. Some norites, such as the banded norite shown above, have interesting igneous layers. Norite also occurs in the highlands of the moon.

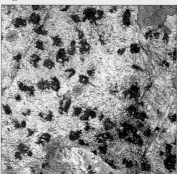

TROCTOLITE

Troctolite is made of large crystals of plagioclase and olivine. This rock was so-named because *troctolite* means "trout-like" and refers to the rock's spots of olivine, which reminded geologists of spotted trout. Troctolite is also found in the highlands of the moon.

111

RHYOLITE
igneous

Rhyolite is made of nearly the same minerals as granite, but the minerals are smaller because rhyolitic lava solidifies quickly on the surface of the earth, rather than slowly below it. Rhyolitic lava is very thick and sticky.

MINERAL COMPOSITION: Quartz, potassium feldspar (sanidine), plagioclase feldspar, biotite, hornblende.

TEXTURE: Fine-grained (small crystals) or glassy.

COLORS: White, gray, pink.

ENVIRONMENT: Rhyolitic lava can erupt violently from volcanoes on continents or ooze out of the ground slowly, forming steep-sided domes.

DACITE

Dacite is a volcanic rock similar to rhyolite. It is made of quartz with plagioclase feldspar (rather than potassium feldspar). Sometimes the crystals are too small to see and it is impossible, even for an expert, to tell dacite from rhyolite. Dacite is the volcanic equivalent of granodiorite and erupts from volcanoes on land, rather than from those under the sea.

ANDESITE

Andesite is the volcanic equivalent of diorite. It has crystals of plagioclase and sometimes hornblende, pyroxene, and biotite. It is the second-most common volcanic rock on earth (basalt is the first), erupting from volcanoes located at the edge of continents. Andesite is named for the Andes Mountains, which were created by andesitic lava flows.

113

Phonolites are volcanic rocks that erupt in places like East Africa's Great Rift Valley, where the continental crust is being torn apart by forces deep within the earth, the same forces that cause earthquakes and volcanic eruptions. Phonolite is the volcanic equivalent of nepheline syenite.

MINERAL COMPOSITION: Potassium feldspar (sanidine), augite, plagioclase, nepheline, sodalite, cancrinite, biotite.

TEXTURE: Fine- to medium-grained or with large crystals of feldspar.

COLORS: Light gray.

ENVIRONMENT: Phonolite forms sheetlike or wall-like masses within rocks (called dikes), as well as lava domes. It forms with other volcanic rocks, such as trachyte (a rock similar to phonolite, but with quartz rather than nepheline, sodalite, or cancrinite), carbonatite, and basalt.

CARBONATITE

Carbonatites are igneous rocks made of carbonate minerals, such as calcite and dolomite. Carbonatites look like limestone and marble, which are also made of calcite.

KIMBERLITE

Kimberlite is a volcanic rock that contains chunks of many different rocks and minerals, including garnets and diamonds. Kimberlites can be gray, greenish, or bluish.

B asalt is the most common volcanic rock on earth. The ocean floor, which makes up two-thirds of the earth's surface, is made of basalt. The dark patches on the moon, called maria ("seas"), are also made of basalt.

MINERAL COMPOSITION: Plagioclase feldspar, pyroxene, sometimes olivine.

TEXTURE: Glassy to fine-grained; some basalt, called vesicular basalt, has holes (vesicles) that were once filled with gas, such as carbon dioxide.

COLORS: Gray to black, dark brown to reddish brown.

ENVIRONMENT: Basalt forms when iron and magnesium-rich lava (which is often thin and runny) solidifies on the surface of a planet.

PILLOW BASALT

When basaltic lava erupts into a lake or sea, it cools very quickly, forming glass on the outside. The molten inside oozes out and cools some more. This lava eventually solidifies into a rounded, pillow-like rock called pillow basalt.

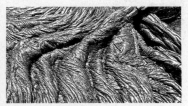

PAHOEHOE

Pahoehoe is ropy-looking basaltic lava that solidifies on land.

DIABASE

Diabase is like basalt, but has larger crystals. It forms from basaltic lava that hardens underground in the cracks through which it travels on its way to the surface.

117

Obsidian is a volcanic rock that forms when lava solidifies so quickly that there is not enough time for crystals to grow. It was used for arrowheads because it can be easily chipped into sharp pieces.

TEXTURE AND MINERAL COMPOSITION: As a rule, obsidian is a glass. It has no mineral crystals. Some types of obsidian, such as snowflake obsidian, have small crystals of feldspar.

COLORS: Obsidian can be a single color (black, brown, or pink), a mixture of colors, or parallel bands of different colors.

ENVIRONMENT: Obsidian usually forms from lava and is found with other volcanic rocks, such as rhyolite, tuff, and pumice.

PUMICE

Like obsidian, pumice is volcanic glass. It forms when gas-rich lava cools instantly. If pumice (named for the Latin word for foam) has enough air space within, it can float on water.

TUFF

Tuff is made up of volcanic ash and glass. Ash-flow tuff forms from flowing avalanches of ash and gas. Air-fall tuff is made of ash that is ejected from a volcano into the air.

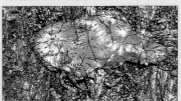

BOMBS

A volcanic bomb is a volcanic rock that is ejected from a volcano and travels through the air before hitting the ground. Bombs with a cracked outer shell are known as "breadcrust bombs."

119

Conglomerate is a sedimentary rock composed of a mixture of rounded pieces of other rocks. Conglomerates can be very colorful, and some contain grains of important minerals, such as gold.

MINERAL COMPOSITION: Almost any mixture of minerals.

TEXTURE: Large, rounded pebbles with finer grains in between.

COLORS: A variety of colors.

ENVIRONMENT: Conglomerate forms from the accumulation of rock fragments that have been rounded by years of traveling through water and air, bumping up against one another. Many conglomerates were once riverbeds or pebbly beaches.

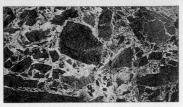

BRECCIA

Breccia is a conglomerate made up of rocks with sharp edges rather than rounded edges. This shows that the rock fragments did not travel very far from the original rock.

IMPACT BRECCIA

Impact breccia is a mixture of fragments of rocks that were hit by a meteorite. Tiny crystals of minerals that form under high pressure can be found in impact breccia.

GLACIAL TILL

Glacial till is a mixture of rocks with different shapes and sizes, from huge boulders to small particles, that were bulldozed into a pile by a glacier.

Many sandstones show clues to the environment they formed in. Layers of sandstone that are hundreds of feet thick formed in deserts. Thinner layers with ripple marks formed in water. Horizontal layers show that the sand accumulated in calm, still water. Diagonal layers (called cross-beds) show which way the wind was blowing or the water was moving.

MINERAL COMPOSITION: Quartz; some with hematite or limonite.

TEXTURE: Fine, sand-sized grains; sometimes has layers of large grains on the bottom and finer grains on top (graded bedding).

COLORS: White, orange, pink, red.

ENVIRONMENT: Sandstone forms when quartz-rich sand along a coast or river or in a desert is buried under layers and layers of more sand and other sediments. Over time, water flowing through the sand grains deposits minerals that cement the sand into rock.

ARKOSE

Arkose is a pinkish rock that forms from eroded granite. It is similar to sandstone but it contains small fragments of feldspar and small rocks as well as quartz. Arkose has sharp or angular corners, showing that it formed near the original granite.

GRAYWACKE

Graywacke is a dark gray to green rock made of quartz, feldspar, and dark-colored rock fragments that are usually volcanic. The mineral grains are sharp and angular, like those of arkose, and they come in a variety of sizes. Graywacke comes from sediment deposited near volcanic rocks.

SHALE
sedimentary

When mud or clay turns to stone, it forms shale. The color of shale depends on the environment in which it formed. Red shales form where there is a lot of oxygen; green and black shales form where there is little oxygen. Some shales are rich in oil.

MINERAL COMPOSITION: Quartz, clay minerals.

TEXTURE: Soft, very fine-grained; may contain fossils.

COLORS: Gray, black, green, red.

ENVIRONMENT: Shale forms when tiny clay particles settle on the bottom of lakes or oceans and are squeezed together by the pressure of other sediment above them.

VARVED CLAY

Varved clays have alternating dark and light layers that were deposited in glacial lakes. The light color represents the summer season; the dark layer represents the winter, when darker particles were laid down.

SILTSTONE

Siltstone has less clay and more quartz than shale, and its grains are slightly larger. Many geologists tell the two apart by their feel: Shale is smooth whereas siltstone is gritty.

125

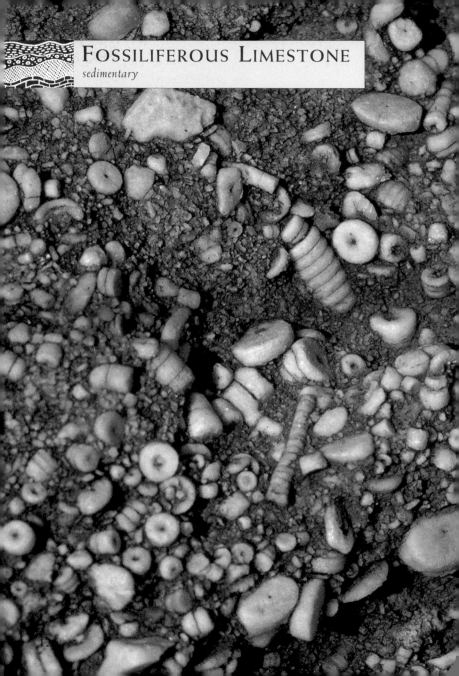

One of the best places to look for fossils is in limestone. Fossiliferous limestone is full of fossils of ancient marine animals that were made of calcium carbonate, including brachiopods, mollusks, and crinoids. Chalk is soft, very fine-grained fossiliferous limestone that is made of the shells of tiny organisms called foraminifera.

MINERAL COMPOSITION: Calcite, dolomite, aragonite.

TEXTURE: Fossils of all sizes with fine-grained calcite in between.

COLORS: White, gray, black, pink.

ENVIRONMENT: Limestone forms in a shallow sea when layers of shells and skeletons of small marine animals become buried and compressed. Over time, the layers turn to rock.

MICRITE

Micrite is very fine-grained limestone that forms from calcite-rich mud deposited in calm, shallow water. Micrite has very few fossils.

OOLITIC/PISOLITIC

Oolitic limestone is made of tiny calcite grains called *oolites* or *ooids*. Oolites form when tiny pieces of shells and rock roll around in a rough, shallow sea and become trapped in layers of calcite.

TRAVERTINE

Travertine is limestone formed in caves. Groundwater flowing through limestone dissolves some of the rock and deposits it in caves, in layers on walls and floors and as droplets that gradually form stalagmites and stalactites

127

Chert is a hard, compact rock made of microscopic quartz crystals. Like obsidian, it breaks into sharp pieces and has been used for arrowheads and cutting tools. Flint is dark gray to black chert found in chalk limestone.

MINERAL COMPOSITION: Quartz, chalcedony.

TEXTURE: Very fine-grained; breaks into curved shapes.

COLORS: Gray, black, green, blue, pink, red, yellow, brown.

ENVIRONMENT: Chert can be found in layers or small, round deposits (nodules) in limestone and chalk where it formed from silica dissolved in water. Some chert is organic, formed of layers of tiny silica animals called radiolaria and diatoms.

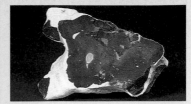

FLINT

Flint is a variety of quartz, usually dark gray, brown, or black in color. It was used by primitive peoples for making tools and weapons.

BANDED IRON FORMATION

This rock is composed of layers of iron-rich materials, such as magnetite, hematite, and jasper.

DIATOMITE

Diatomite is made of the shells of diatoms, tiny marine animals that accumulated on the sea floor. Diatomite is white, fine-grained, soft, light, and full of tiny holes (porous).

ANTHRACITE COAL
sedimentary/metamorphic

Anthracite is the highest-grade, purest form of coal. It has the most carbon in it and burns the best. Because anthracite takes so much pressure, heat, and time to form, it is generally found only in rock formations more than 65 million years old.

MINERAL COMPOSITION: Coal is made of plant material (which is made of compounds known as "macerals"), rather than minerals. Coal may also contain small amounts of pyrite, sand, and clay.

TEXTURE: Smooth; breaks into pieces that are flat on the top and bottom.

COLOR: Shiny black.

ENVIRONMENT: Coal is found in sedimentary rocks, between layers of other rocks such as sandstone, limestone, and shale. Sometimes the layers are flat, and sometimes they are wavy.

PEAT
Peat is dead plant matter that has accumulated in swampy areas and has begun to decompose.

LIGNITE
Lignite is a soft brown, low-grade form of coal. It forms when peat is buried and compressed.

BITUMINOUS COAL
Bituminous is brownish-black coal. It forms when lignite is subject to great pressure over time. With even more pressure and time, bituminous coal becomes anthracite.

131

SLATE
metamorphic

Slate breaks into smooth, flat sheets and is therefore very useful for making blackboards, floors, and roofs. The color of slate—black, gray, green, or red—depends on the color of the shale from which it is formed.

MINERAL COMPOSITION: Mica, quartz, sometimes pyrite.

TEXTURE: Very fine-grained; crystals are arranged in flat sheets.

COLORS: Red, green, gray, black, multicolored.

ENVIRONMENT: Slate forms when shale is buried, squeezed, and heated. It is common in mountainous regions of North America.

PHYLLITE

When slate is metamorphosed, the mica grains grow, giving a silky sheen to the resulting rock, known as phyllite. Like slate, phyllite is easily split into fairly flat sheets. Some phyllites have very fine waves or folds, called crenulations, in the rock. The grains in phyllite are visible under a magnifying glass, but not to the naked eye.

HORNFELS

Hot magma can bake the older, cooler rocks it flows through, forming a metamorphic rock called hornfels. Its mineral composition and grain size depend on what the original rock was and how hot and how long it was heated.

133

MICA SCHIST
metamorphic

Mica schist is easily identified by its sparkly mica grains. Because the grains are larger than those in slate and phyllite, schist doesn't break as cleanly, but it breaks more easily than gneiss.

MINERAL COMPOSITION: Biotite or muscovite mica, quartz, feldspar.

TEXTURE: Medium- to coarse-grained; grains are arranged in parallel sheets.

COLORS: Sparkly gray to black.

ENVIRONMENT: Schist is found in old and young mountain ranges. It forms when slate that has metamorphosed to phyllite is put under even more heat and pressure.

GARNET SCHIST

Garnet schist contains garnets, usually almandine, as well as mica, quartz, and feldspar. Most garnet schists are metamorphic rocks that were once muddy and sandy sediments.

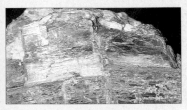

KYANITE SCHIST

Kyanite schist contains flat, blade-like crystals of blue or yellow kyanite, as well as quartz, mica, and feldspar. Kyanite schist needs extremely high pressure to form.

BLUESCHIST

Blueschist forms when rocks such as graywacke and basalt are subjected to very high pressure.

135

BANDED GNEISS
metamorphic

B anded gneiss has distinct light and dark layering. If you look at a large section of bedrock (an outcrop), such as a mountain or a rocky ridge along a highway, you may also see that the layers are wavy (folded).

MINERAL COMPOSITION: Quartz and feldspar in the light layers; biotite, hornblende, augite, enstatite in the dark layers.

TEXTURE: Large grains; interlocking crystals; layered; harder to break than schist.

COLORS: Multicolored: black, white, pink, green.

ENVIRONMENT: Gneiss forms when other rocks have been metamorphosed at high temperature and pressure for a long time. Because it forms very deep in the earth's crust, gneiss can only be seen in mountain chains where the rock has been uplifted or where the rock over it has eroded away.

GRANITIC GNEISS

Granitic gneiss was once granite. It is like granite in color and mineral composition, but the minerals are usually divided into light quartz- and feldspar-rich areas and darker biotite-rich areas.

AUGEN GNEISS

This gneiss has large eye-shaped crystals of feldspar, surrounded by smaller biotite, feldspar, and quartz crystals. *Augen* is the German word for "eye."

MIGMATITE

Migmatite means "mixed rock." Many migmatites appear to be gneisses that got so hot they melted in some places and are now mixtures of gneiss and granite.

137

Eclogite is sometimes called Christmas tree rock because it is green and spotted with round, red garnets. Some eclogites contain diamonds.

MINERAL COMPOSITION: Pyrope garnet, pyroxene, sometimes kyanite.

TEXTURE: Medium-grained.

COLORS: Green, red.

ENVIRONMENT: Eclogite is a rock that forms very deep in the earth under very high temperature and pressure. Some eclogites are metamorphosed basalts; others may be igneous rocks. Eclogite can be seen in huge areas where the rock above it has eroded away or in small, rounded, or flat pieces that were ejected during volcanic eruptions.

AMPHIBOLITE

Amphibolite is a dark green to black, coarse-grained rock made of hornblende and other amphibole minerals. It forms when basalt is metamorphosed. You may be looking at an ancient lava flow when you see amphibolite.

SERPENTINITE

Serpentinite is a relatively soft, green rock made of the mineral serpentine. Some huge serpentinite rocks were once part of the basalt and gabbro layers of the ocean crust. Serpentinite is used as a building stone (called "verde antique").

139

MARBLE
metamorphic

Marble occurs in a variety of colors, depending on the purity of the original limestone. If the limestone was pure, the marble is white; if there were impurities, the marble can be black, green, red, or yellow-brown; if the impurities were spread out unevenly, the marble is spotty or "marbled." Because marble is soft but sturdy, it has been a popular building and carving stone through the ages. Unfortunately, like limestone, marble slowly disintegrates in acid rain.

MINERAL COMPOSITION: Calcite, dolomite, small amounts of metamorphic minerals.

TEXTURE: Fine- to-coarse-grained.

COLORS: White, gray, black, pink, blue; often streaked.

ENVIRONMENT: Marble forms when limestone is metamorphosed, usually when mountains are being formed.

QUARTZITE

Quartzite is mostly made of quartz. It forms when buried sandstone is heated, forcing the quartz grains tightly together. From far away, quartzite may look just like sandstone, with horizontal and diagonal layers. Quartzite is much harder than sandstone because the crystals are interlocking, with almost no space between them.

METAMORPHOSED CONGLOMERATE

When conglomerate is metamorphosed, the pebbles are squashed into flattened ovals and ribbons. Metamorphosed conglomerate is much harder than sedimentary conglomerate because quartz and other minerals fill in all the spaces that were once filled only with air.

141

Chondrites are the oldest known rocks in the solar system. They formed at the beginning of the solar system (4.55 billion years ago) and contain clues about its age and composition. Chondrites are made of chondrules, which are tiny, round, igneous rocks that melted by a mysterious process while floating in space.

MINERAL COMPOSITION: Olivine, pyroxene, plagioclase feldspar, magnetite, calcite, dolomite, siderite, and other minerals that are rare on earth (such as troilite).

TEXTURE: Round chondrules with broken chondrules and other small mineral fragments.

COLOR: Gray.

ENVIRONMENT: Chondrites and other meteorites that have recently fallen to earth have a black crust, which shows that the outside of the meteorites melted as they fell through the atmosphere.

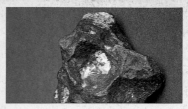

IRON METEORITE

Iron meteorites are very dense rocks made of iron-nickel minerals and an iron sulfide mineral called troilite. They come from the inner cores of asteroids.

PALLASITE

Pallasites are meteorites made of iron-nickel minerals and green olivine crystals. They formed within an asteroid between the core and the mantle.

TEKTITE

Tektites are black or greenish pieces of natural glass. Tektites form when a meteorite hits the earth and melts the rock it collides with. Some pieces cool into streamlined shapes, others solidify as squashed droplets.

143

How to use the reference section

Labradorite

The **Glossary** below contains terms used by geologists. Following it is a **Table of Minerals**, indicating the chemical groupings for important minerals in the field guide. After the table are lists of rock-and-mineral **Resources**—books, tapes, CDs, and organizations. Finally, there is an **Index** of rocks and minerals covered in the guide.

Acid rain
Rain that contains a large amount of chemicals from factories, cars, and other sources of pollution, which can harm or destroy living and nonliving things on earth.

Amber
Tree sap that has been buried and then hardened into rock.

Pyrolusite

Amphiboles
A group of silicate minerals that form in many igneous and metamorphic rocks. The amphiboles include actinolite and hornblende.

Angular rocks
Rocks with sharp, not rounded, edges. Angular rocks are found near the rocks they broke off from.

Atom
The smallest particle of a chemical element that can exist by itself or in combination with other elements.

Basalt
A dark volcanic rock rich in iron and magnesium minerals. Basalt is the most

common volcanic rock on earth. The ocean floor is made of basalt.

Bedrock
Solid rock underlying loose rocks, soil, and sediment.

Bladed crystals
Crystals that are shaped-like the blade of a knife—flat, broad, and narrower on one end.

Branching crystals
Crystals that are shaped like the branches of a tree. Also called "arborescent."

Breccia
Sedimentary rock containing a mixture of angular (with sharp edges) fragments of other rocks.

Carbon
An element found in all organic (living) and many inorganic (nonliving) things.

Carbonate
The molecule CO_3. Carbonate minerals, including calcite and siderite, are those that contain CO_3. Carbonate rocks, such as limestone and marble, are made of carbonate minerals.

Chemical composition
The amounts of different elements that a particular mineral or rock is made of.

Chemical formula
Symbols that tell how many atoms of each element a particular mineral is made of. For instance, the chemical formula for Quartz is SiO_2; quartz is made of one atom of silicon for every two atoms of oxygen.

Cleavage
The tendency of some minerals to crack or break along flat surfaces, or planes.

Cleavage Plane, or Cleavage Surface
The flat broken surface of a mineral.

Compound
A combination of two or more elements bonded together. For instance, water (H_2O).

Conchoidal fracture
A curved broken surface of a mineral or rock. The shape of the break (fracture) resembles a seashell.

Continental crust
The part of the earth's crust that includes the continents. It is lighter and thicker than oceanic crust.

Core
The metallic center of the earth. The inner core is solid, and scientists believe it is made of iron and nickel; the outer core is liquid.

Cross-bedded Navajo sandstone

GLOSSARY

Garnet schist

Crust

The outermost layer of the earth. It ranges in thickness from about 3 to 40 miles.

Crystal

An element or compound (can be a mineral, a man-made mineral, or an organic substance) with an external geometric shape.

Crystalline substance

A material whose atoms are arranged in a regular, three-dimensional pattern that is repeated throughout the material. All minerals have a crystalline structure.

Density

The mass of a substance per unit of volume. Density is often measured in grams per cubic centimeter. If two objects are the same size, the denser object weighs more.

Dike

A sheet or wall-like mass of igneous rock that cuts across other rocks.

Element

The simplest substance, one that contains only one kind of atom. Examples are oxygen, hydrogen, carbon, and gold.

Erosion

The wearing down and transport of rocks as a result of forces such as wind, water, heating, freezing, and gravity.

Feldspar minerals

A group of silicate minerals that are the most important rock-forming minerals.

Feldspar minerals, which include plagioclase and orthoclase, are rich in potassium, aluminum, calcium, and sodium as well as silicon and oxygen.

Feldspathoid minerals

A group of silicate minerals, including nepheline and sodalite, that are similar to the feldspars, but which contain less silica.

Fossil

The remains or outline of an ancient plant or animal preserved in rock.

146

Gypsum cliffs

Kimberlite

Fracture
A rough or uneven break in a mineral.

Gemstones
Minerals such as diamonds, emeralds, or rubies that can be made into jewels when cut and polished. Gemstones that are very valuable (because they are beautiful, long-lasting, and somewhat rare) are called precious gems. Less valuable stones such as garnet are called semi-precious gems.

Geologist
A scientist who studies rocks and minerals, the processes that form rocks, minerals, and landscapes, and the history of the earth and other planets.

Hardness
The resistance of a mineral to being scratched. Hardness is rated on Mohs' Hardness Scale which ranges from 1, the softest, to 10, the hardest.

Igneous rock
One of the three main types of rock on earth. Igneous rocks form when magma cools either on the surface of the earth (volcanic rock) or deep within the earth (plutonic rock). Basalt is a volcanic igneous rock; granite is a plutonic igneous rock.

Lava
Lava is the name given to magma (molten or melted rock) when it reaches the earth's surface. It is ejected from volcanoes during eruptions or oozes from cracks in the earth's surface.

Magma
Molten (melted or liquid) rock underneath the earth's surface.

Mantle
The hot, solid layer of the earth between the crust and the core. Most of the volume of the earth is mantle.

Metamorphic rock
Rocks such as slate and marble that form when other rocks have been heated and/or put under pressure.

Mineral
A solid element or compound that occurs in nature and has a specific chemical composition and a definite crystal structure. Most minerals are formed by geological processes rather than by living things.

Mineraloid
A natural material, such as opal, that is technically not a mineral because it either doesn't have a definite structure or doesn't have a definite chemical composition.

Molecule
The smallest unit of a chemical compound.

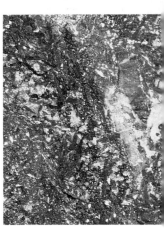

Cinnabar

GLOSSARY

Native elements
Elements that occur by themselves, not in combination with other elements. Native elements include gold, silver, platinum, carbon, and sulfur.

Oceanic crust
The part of the earth's crust that lies beneath the oceans. Oceanic crust is denser and thinner than continental crust.

Ore
A concentration of a useful element or material, that can be mined for profit. A mineral or rock that potentially contains a significant amount of a useful element. For example, galena is an ore of lead, and hematite is an iron ore.

Organic substance
A substance formed by living things or that makes up living things.

Outcrop
A rock formation that is exposed on the earth's surface.

Paleontologist
A scientist who studies fossils and prehistoric life-forms.

Pegmatite
An igneous rock with very large crystals. Pegmatites usually occur as dikes that cut across other igneous rocks, usually granite.

Petrified Wood
Wood that has been replaced by minerals and therefore turned to stone.

Plutonic rock
An igneous rock formed by magma that cooled and solidified below the earth's surface. Its grains are coarser than those of volcanic rock.

Prismatic crystal
A crystal with one dimension longer than the other two. For instance, a column.

Pyroxenes
A group of silicate minerals, such as augite and enstatite, are essential components of many rocks. They all have the molecule (Si_2O6) in their chemical formula. Pyroxenes are most commonly found in igneous rocks.

Quartz
The most common mineral in the earth's crust. It's found in sedimentary, igneous, and metamorphic rocks.

Rock
A hard, solid mass composed of one or more minerals or other elements or compounds.

Sand
Small grains of eroded or disintegrated rock. Most sand is composed of minerals such as quartz that are hard and don't dissolve or decompose easily.

Sediment
Pieces or small particles of rock, soil, sand, shells, animal skeletons, and plant remains that accumulate on the surface of the earth: for example at bottom of a river, lake, pond, or ocean, at the base of a mountain, or in a desert. Examples are pebbles, sand, and clay.

Sedimentary
Sedimentary rocks are one

Ulexite crystals

Seams of coal

of the three main types of rocks on earth. They form when sediments lithify, or turn into rock.

Silica
The compound SiO_2, silicon dioxide.

Silicates
Minerals that contain silicon and oxygen. The majority of common rock-forming minerals are silicates.

Specific gravity
The weight of a mineral divided by the weight of an equal volume of water. Specific gravity is equivalent to density.

Stalactites
Cone- or column-shaped forms that grow down from a cave ceiling. Stalactites are usually made of calcite.

Stalagmites
Cone-shaped forms that grow up from the floor of a cave. Stalagmites are usually made of calcite.

Realgar crystals

Streak
The color of a mineral when it is ground into a powder or rubbed across a tile of unglazed white porcelain known as a "streak plate."

Striations
Parallel grooves on the surface of a crystal surface or cleavage surface of a mineral.

Volcanic rock
Igneous rock, such as basalt, that is formed when magma cools and solidifies quickly near or on the earth's surface rather than within the earth.

149

TABLE OF MINERALS

An element is the simplest kind of substance, containing only one kind of atom. In a chemical formula, each element is abbreviated with a symbol. Some symbols, such as S for sulfur, are easy to understand. Others, like Pb for lead, seem strange. These are usually based on the Latin or Greek names for the elements.

Every mineral is made up of molecules: one or more atoms of different elements that are bonded together chemically. The chemical formula of a mineral tells how many atoms of each element are in one molecule. For instance, the chemical formula for quartz is SiO_2. This means that quartz contains one atom of silicon (Si) for every two atoms of oxygen (O).

The formula for olivine is $(Fe,Mg)_2SiO_4$. The comma between the Fe (iron) and Mg (magnesium) means that there a total of two atoms of iron and magnesium in each molecule. Some olivine molecules have two atoms of iron, some have two atoms of magnesium, and some have one atom of iron and one atom of magnesium. All olivine molecules have one atom of silicon and four atoms of oxygen.

Some minerals have water (H_2O) in their structure. The formula for gypsum—$CaSO_4 \cdot 2H_2O$—tells us that gypsum is made of one atom of calcium, one atom of sulfur, four atoms of oxygen, and two molecules of water. In a few cases, a chemical formula says "nH_2O". This means that there is water in the mineral, but the exact amount is unknown or differs from specimen to specimen.

The minerals listed below are grouped according to chemical type or occurrence. The names of the groups are given in bold.

MINERAL	FORMULA	MINERAL	FORMULA
NATIVE METALS		Ilmenite	$FeTiO_3$
Gold	Au	Hematite	Fe_2O_3
Silver	Ag	Limonite	$FeO(OH) \cdot nH_2O$
Platinum	Pt	Goethite	$FeO \cdot OH$
CARBON POLYMORPHS		**OXIDES**	
Diamond	C	Corundum	Al_2O_3
Graphite	C	Spinel	$MgAl_2O_4$
COPPER MINERALS		Sapphire	Al_2O_3
Copper	Cu	Rutile	TiO_2
Azurite	$Cu_3(CO_3)_2(OH)_2$	**RADIOACTIVE MINERALS**	
Malachite	$Cu_2CO_3(OH)_2$	Uraninite	UO_2
Bornite	Cu_5FeS_4	Autunite	$Ca(UO_2)_2(PO_4)_2 \cdot 8\text{-}12$
IRON-SULFIDES		Zircon	$ZrSiO_4$
Pyrite	FeS_2	Monazite	$(Ce,La,Y,Th)PO_4$
Marcasite	FeS_2	**MANGANESE MINERALS**	
Chalcopyrite	$CuFeS_2$	Rhodochrosite	$MnCO_3$
Pyrrhotite	$Fe_{(1-x)}S$	Rhodonite	$MnSiO_3$
LEAD-ZINC MINERALS		Pyrolusite	MnO_2
Galena	PbS	Manganite	$MnO(OH)$
Sphalerite	ZnS	**CARBONATE MINERALS**	
Cerussite	$PbCO_3$	Calcite	$CaCO_3$
Wulfenite	$PbMoO_4$	Aragonite	$CaCO_3$
IRON OXIDES		Dolomite	$CaMg(CO_3)_2$
Magnetite	Fe_3O_4	Siderite	$FeCO_3$
Chromite	$FeCr_2O_4$		

TABLE OF MINERALS

MINERAL	FORMULA	MINERAL	FORMULA
FLUORITE MINERALS		**PYROXENES**	
Fluorite	CaF_2	Augite	$(Ca,Na)(Mg,Fe,Al)$
Barite	$BaSO_4$		$(Si,Al)_2O_6$
Apatite	$Ca_5(PO_4)_3(F,OH,Cl)$	Jadeite	$NaAlSi_2O_6$
SALTS		Spodumene	$LiAlSi_2O_6$
Halite	$NaCl$	**AMPHIBOLES**	
Sylvite	KCl	Actinolite	$Ca_2(Mg,Fe)_5$
Epsomite	$MgSO_4 \cdot 7H_2O$		$Si_8O_{22}(OH)_2$
EVAPORITE MINERALS		Nephrite Jade	$Ca_2(Mg,Fe)_5Si_8$
Gypsum	$CaSO4 \cdot 2H_2O$		$O_{22}(OH)_2$
Anhydrite	$CaSO_4$	Hornblende	$(Ca,Na)_{2\text{-}3}(Mg,Fe,Al)_5$
Sulfur	S		$Si_6(Si,Al)_2O_{22}(OH)_2$
BORON MINERALS		**MICAS**	
Borax	$Na_2B_4O_5(OH)_4 \cdot 8H_2O$	Muscovite Mica	$KAl_2(AlSi_3O_{10})(OH)_2$
Ulexite	$NaCaB_5O_6(OH)_6 \cdot$	Biotite	$K(Mg,Fe)_3(AlSi_3O_{10})$
	$5H2O$		$(OH,F)_2$
Colemanite	$CaB_3O_4(OH)_3 \cdot H_2O$	Lepidolite	$K(Li,Fe,Al)_3(Si,Al)_4$
QUARTZ			$O_{10}(OH,F)_2$
Quartz	SiO_2	Margarite	$CaAl_2(Al_2Si_2O_{10})(OH)_2$
Amethyst	SiO_2	**CLAY MINERALS**	
Rose Quartz	SiO_2	Vermiculite	$Mg_3Si_4O_{10}\text{-}(OH)_2 \cdot$
Milky Quartz	SiO_2		nH_2O
Herkimer Diamond	SiO_2	Kaolinite	$Al_2Si_2O_5(OH)_4$
SILICA MINERALS		Montmorillonite	$(Na_2,Ca)(Al,Mg)_2(Si_4O_{10})$
Opal	$SiO_2 \cdot nH_2O$		$(OH)_2 \cdot nH_2O$
Chalcedony	SiO_2	**PHYLLO SILICATES**	
Jasper	SiO_2	Talc	$Mg_3Si_4O_{10}(OH)_2$
POTASSIUM FELDSPARS		Pyrophyllite	$Al_2Si_4O_{10}(OH)_2$
Orthoclase	$KAlSi_3O_8$	Serpentine	$Mg_3Si_2O_5(OH)_4$
Sanidine	$KAlSi_3O_8$	**OLIVINE**	
Microcline	$KAlSi_3O_8$	Olivine	$(Mg,Fe)_2SiO_4$
PLAGIOCLASE FELDSPARS		Diopside	$CaMgSi_2O_6$
Albite	$NaAlSi_3O_8$	Epidote	$Ca_2(Al,Fe)Al_2O(SiO_4)$
Labradorite	$CaAl_2Si_2O_8 - NaAlSi_3O_8$		$(Si_2O_7)(OH)$
Anorthite	$CaAl_2Si_2O_8$	**METAMORPHIC INDICATORS**	
FELDSPATHOIDS		Staurolite	$Fe_2Al_9O_6(SiO_4)_4$
Lazurite	$(Na,Ca)_4(AlSiO_4)_3$		$(O,OH)_2$
	(SO_4,S,Cl)	Andalusite	Al_2SiO_5
Sodalite	$Na_4(AlSiO_4)_3Cl$	Kyanite	Al_2SiO_5
Nepheline	$(Na,K)AlSiO_4$	Sillimanite	Al_2SiO_5
ZEOLITES		**GARNETS**	
Natrolite	$Na_2Al_2Si_3O_{10} \cdot 2H_2O$	Almandine	$Fe_3Al_2Si_3O_{12}$
Heulandite	$CaAl_2Si_7O_{18} \cdot 6H_2O$	Pyrope	$Mg_3Al_2Si_3O_{12}$
Stilbite	$NaCa_2Al_5Si_{13}O_{36} \cdot$	Grossular	$Ca_3Al_2Si_3O_{12}$
	$14H_2O$	Spessartine	$Mn_3Al_2Si_3O_{12}$
Chabazite	$CaAl_2Si_4O_{12} \cdot 6H_2O$		
PEGMATITE GEMS			
Beryl	$Be_3Al_2Si_6O_{18}$		
Tourmaline	$(Na,Ca)(Li,Mg,Al)$		
	$(Al,Fe,Mn)_6(BO_3)_3$		
	$Si_6O_{18}(OH)_4$		
Topaz	$Al_2SiO_4(F_1OH)_2$		

RESOURCES

FOR FURTHER READING

Geology
Boy Scouts of America, 1985

Geology
(Golden Guide)
Frank H. T. Rhodes
Golden Press, 1991

Snowflake obsidian

How the Earth Works
John Farndon
Reader's Digest Association, Inc., 1992

Incredible Earth: A Book of Answers for Kids
Ann-Jeanette Cambell and Ronald Rood
John Wiley & Sons, Inc., 1996

Introduction to Rocks and Minerals
Dougal Dixon
Book Sales, Inc., 1996

It Could Still Be a Rock (Rookie Read-about Science Series)
Allan Fowler
Children's Press, 1993

Let's Go Rock Collecting
(Let's-Read-And-Find-Out Science Series: Stage 1)
Roma Gans and Holly Keller (Illustrator)
HarperCollins,1996

National Audubon Society Field Guide to North American Rocks and Minerals
Charles W. Chesterman and Kurt E. Lowe
Alfred A. Knopf, 1995

National Audubon Society Pocket Guide to Familiar Rocks and Minerals of
North America
Charles W. Chesterman
Alfred A. Knopf, 1995

Rocks
(Golden Science Close-up Series)
Golden Press, 1991

Rocks
(Threads Series)
Terry J. Jennings
Garrett Education Corporation, 1991

Rocks
(Earth in Action Series)
Tom Mariner
Marshall Cavendish, 1990

Rocks
Gregg Quinn
Scholastic Inc., 1995

Rocks
(Voyages Series)
Judy Tuer
SRA Schl. Group., 1993

Rocks and Fossils
(Nature Company Guide Series)
Arthur Bresnahan Busbey
Time-Life, 1996

Rocks and Fossils
(Hobby Guides Series)
B. Cork and M. Bramwell
EDC Publishing, 1983

Rocks and Minerals
(Discover Series)
Publications International Ltd., 1993

Rocks and Minerals
(Pocket Guides Series)
Firefly Bks Ltd., 1996

Rocks and Minerals
Joel Arem
Geoscience Press, 1991

Rocks and Minerals
(Nature Fact Book)
D.J. Arneson and Howard Friedman (Illustrator)
Kidsbooks, 1990

Rocks and Minerals
(Macmillan Field Guides)
Pat Bell and David Wright
Collier Books, 1985

Rocks and Minerals
(DK Pocket Series)
Sue Fuller
DK Publishing, 1995

Rocks and Minerals
(Question & Answer Books)
Elizabeth Marcus
Troll Communications, 1983

Rocks and Minerals
(Eyewitness Books)
Natural History Museum Staff
Alfred A. Knopf Books for Young Readers, 1988

Rocks and Minerals
(At Your Fingertips Series)
Judy Nayer
McClanahan Books, 1995

152

Rocks and Minerals
Mary Packard
Troll Communications,
1995

Rocks and Minerals
(Eyewitness Handbooks)
Chris Pellant
DK Publishing,
1992

Rocks and Minerals
(Fact Finders Series)
Chris Pellant
Random House,
1990

Rocks and Minerals
(Peterson First Guides)
Frederick H. Pough
Houghton Mifflin Company,
1991

Rocks and Minerals
(Science Nature Guide Series)
Theodore Rowland-Entwistle
and Michael O'Donoghue
Thunder Bay, 1994

Rocks and Minerals
(From This Earth Series)
William Russell
Rourke Corporation,
1994

Rocks and Minerals
Charles A. Sorrel
Golden Press, 1973

Rocks and Minerals
(Spotter's Guides Series)
Alan Woolley
EDC Publishing,
1992

Rocks, Minerals, and Fossils
(Our World Series)
Keith Lye
Silver Burdett Press,
1991

ORGANIZATIONS

American Museum of Natural History
175-208 Central Park West
New York, NY 10024
Tel: 212-769-5100
//research.amnh.org/earthplan/ind
ex.html

San Francisco Gem and Mineral Society
4134 Judah Street
San Francisco, CA 94122
Tel: 415-564-4230
e-mail: Jeffiner@pobox.com
//www.sfgms.org/

Smithsonian Museum of Natural History
2 Massachusetts Avenue, NE
Washington, DC 20002-4225
Tel: 202-357-1300

United States Geological Survey
12201 Sunrise Valley Drive
National Center
Reston, VA 20191
Tel: 703-648-7411
//www.usgs.gov/

The Ventura Gem and Mineral Society, Inc.
P.O. Box 1573
Ventura, CA 93002
Tel: 1-805-648-4051
e-mail: jns@west.net
//www.west.net/~jns/vgms/

WEB SITES

Geoscience: K–12 Resources
www.cuug.ab.ca:8001/~johnstos/
geosci.html

A Homepage for Rock Hounds
Zimmer.csufresno.edu/~khperen/
geology.htm

Rockhound Information Page
www.rahul.net/infodyn/rockhoun
ds/rockhounds.html

Rocks and Minerals (Koday's Kid's Home Page)
www.willowgrove.district96.K12.
il.us/Rocks and
Minerals/rocks.html

Smithsonian Gem and Mineral Collection
galaxy.einet/images/gems/gems-
icons.html

Yahoo Resource For Rocks, Gems And Minerals
www.yahoo.com/recreation/hobb
ies_and_crafts/rocks_gems_and_
minerals/

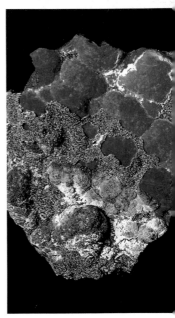

Malachite/azurite

INDEX

Limestone

Bornite

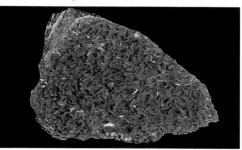

PHOTO/ILLUSTRATION CREDITS

Credits are listed by page, from left to right, top to bottom.

1 Martin Land/SPL/Photo Researchers, Inc.
2–3 Rod Planck/Photo Researchers, Inc.
4–5 Biophoto Associates/Photo Researchers, Inc.
6 George Whiteley/Photo Researchers, Inc.
8a Courtesy of Portraits Collection/USGS
8b William H. Mullins/Photo Researchers, Inc.
10a Breck P. Kent
10b Biophoto Associates/Photo Researchers, Inc.
11a Gregory G. Dimijian/Photo Researchers, Inc.
11b E.R. Degginger/Photo Researchers, Inc.
11c Dr. Paul Zahl/Photo Researchers, Inc.
12–13 (Earth) Lynette Cook/SPL/Photo Researchers, Inc.
13a Dr. E.R. Degginger
13b John W. Bova/Photo Researchers, Inc.
13c Ray Ellis/Photo Researchers, Inc.
13d Lawrence Migdale/Photo Researchers, Inc.
14–15 (volcano) Soames Summerhays/Photo Researchers, Inc.
14 George Bernard/SPL/Photo Researchers, Inc.
15a Betty Derig/Photo Researchers, Inc.
15b George Whiteley/Photo Researchers, Inc.
16 Soames Summerhays/Photo Researchers, Inc.
17a Tim Davis/Photo Researchers, Inc.
17b Calvin Larsen/Photo Researchers, Inc.
17c John R. Foster
18a John Buitenkant/Photo Researchers, Inc.
18b George E. McGill
19a (Devil's Tower) James Hanley/Photo Researchers, Inc.
19b John R. Foster
19c Ken M. Johns/Photo Researchers, Inc.
20–21 (background) Phillip Hayson/Photo Researchers, Inc.
20a Phillip Hayson/Photo Researchers, Inc.
20b Andrew J. Martinez
20c B. Walsh, J. Beckett, M. Carruthers*
21a B. Walsh, J. Beckett, M. Carruthers*
21b Dr. E.R. Degginger
21c Andrew J. Martinez
21d B. Walsh, J. Beckett, M Carruthers*
22–23 Gregory G. Dimijian/Photo Researchers, Inc.
23a Michael P. Gadomski/Photo Researchers, Inc.
23b Michael P. Gadomski/Photo Researchers, Inc.
23c Mark C. Burnett/Photo Researchers, Inc.
23d Mark C. Burnett/Photo Researchers, Inc.
24–25 (background) Charles R. Belinky/Photo Researchers, Inc.
24a Charles R. Belinky/Photo Researchers, Inc.
24b Joyce Photographics/Photo Researchers, Inc.
24c Russell D. Curtis/Photo Researchers, Inc.
25a Alan & Linda Detrick
25b Ken M. Johns/Photo Researchers, Inc.
26–27 (background) Tom McHugh/Photo Researchers, Inc.

26a E.R. Degginger/Photo Researchers, Inc.
26b Arthur R. Hill/Visuals Unlimited
26c Joyce Photographics/Photo Researchers, Inc.
27a B. Walsh, J. Beckett, M. Carruthers*
27b Breck P. Kent
27c Bill Bachmann/Photo Researchers, Inc.
28–29 (background) Adam Hart-Davis/SPL/Photo Researchers, Inc.
28a Joy Spurr
28b E.R. Degginger/Photo Researchers, Inc.
29a M. Claye/Jacana/Photo Researchers, Inc.
29b Lincoln Nutting/Photo Researchers, Inc.
29c Ray Simons/Photo Researchers, Inc.
29d Andrew J. Martinez/Photo Researchers, Inc.
29e Wolfgang Vogt
29f George Whiteley/Photo Researchers, Inc.
29g Dr. E.R. Degginger
29h B. Walsh, J. Beckett, M. Carruthers*
30–31 (realgar) E.R. Degginger/Photo Researchers, Inc.
30a Gary Retherford/Photo Researchers, Inc.
30b Charles D. Winters
30c Charles D. Winters
30d Thomas R. Taylor/Photo Researchers, Inc.
30e Breck P. Kent
30f E.R. Degginger/Photo Researchers, Inc.
31a Kathleen A. Blanchard/Visuals Unlimited
31b Thomas R. Taylor/Photo Researchers, Inc.
31c Joyce Photographics/Photo Researchers, Inc.
32a Breck P. Kent
32b Breck P. Kent
32c Louise K. Broman/Photo Researchers, Inc.
32d Charles D. Winters
33a Breck P. Kent
33b Gilbert S. Grant/Photo Researchers, Inc.
33c Joyce Photographics/Photo Researchers, Inc.
33d George Whiteley/Photo Researchers, Inc.
33e Andrew J. Martinez
33f Biophoto Associates/Photo Researchers, Inc.
34a (talc) Andrew J. Martinez
34b (gypsum) Charles D. Winters
34c (calcite) E.R. Degginger/Photo Researchers, Inc.
34d (fluorite) E.R. Degginger/Photo Researchers, Inc.
34e (apatite) Breck P. Kent
35a (orthoclase) Biophoto Associates/Photo Researchers, Inc.
35b (quartz) Andrew J. Martinez
35c (topaz) M. Claye/Jacana/Photo Researchers, Inc.
35d (corundum) Charles D. Winters/Photo Researchers, Inc.
35e (diamond) Breck P. Kent
35f J. Gerard Smith/Photo Researchers, Inc.
36a Charles D. Winters
36b Biophoto Associates/Photo Researchers, Inc.
36c Biophoto Associates/Photo Researchers, Inc.
37a George Holton/Photo Researchers, Inc.
37b Ken Eward/BioGrafx/Photo Researchers, Inc.

PHOTO/ILLUSTRATION CREDITS

37c   Ken Eward/BioGrafx/Photo Researchers, Inc.
37d   Phillip Hatson/Photo Researchers, Inc.
38–39 (fossil shells) John R. Foster
38a   James L. Amos/Photo Researchers, Inc.
38b   François Gohier/Photo Researchers, Inc.
39a   John Reader/SPL/Photo Researchers, Inc.
39b   François Gohier/Photo Researchers, Inc.
40a   John Cancalosi
40b   Science VU/Visuals Unlimited
40c   Ludek Pesek/SPL/Photo Researchers, Inc.
41a   Lowell Georgia/Photo Researchers, Inc.
41b   Noah Poritz/MacroWorld/Photo Researchers, Inc.
41c   A.J. Copley/Visuals Unlimited
41d   John Cancalosi/Potomac Museum Group
42a   Charles D. Winters
42b   Gregory G. Dimijian/Photo Researchers, Inc.
44   Tom McHugh/Photo Researchers, Inc.
45a   Paolo Koch/Photo Researchers, Inc.
45b   E.R. Degginger/Color-Pic, Inc.
46   Breck P. Kent
47a   Andrew J. Martinez/Photo Researchers, Inc.
47b   Dr. E.R. Degginger
48   Tom McHugh/Photo Researchers, Inc.
49a   Charles D. Winters/Photo Researchers, Inc.
49b   Vaughan Fleming/SPL/Photo Researchers, Inc.
49c   Biophoto Associates/Photo Researchers, Inc.
50   Gary Retherford/Photo Researchers, Inc.
51a   Joyce Photographics/Photo Researchers, Inc.
51b   Joyce Photographics/Photo Researchers, Inc.
51c   Wolfgang Vogt
52   E.R. Degginger/Photo Researchers, Inc.
53a   Wolfgang Vogt
53b   Tom McHugh/Photo Researchers, Inc.
53c   E.R. Degginger/Photo Researchers, Inc.
54   Tom McHugh/Photo Researchers, Inc.
55a   Biophoto Associates/Photo Researchers, Inc.
55b   Charles D. Winters/Photo Researchers, Inc.
56   Charles R. Belinky/Photo Researchers, Inc.
57a   E.R. Degginger/Color-Pic, Inc.
57b   B. Walsh, J. Beckett, M. Carruthers*
58   Charles D. Winters/Photo Researchers, Inc.
59a   Wolfgang Vogt
59b   Biophoto Associates/Photo Researchers, Inc.
59c   George Whiteley/Photo Researchers, Inc.
60   Tom McHugh/Photo Researchers, Inc.
61a   Ray Simons/Photo Researchers, Inc.
61b   Breck P. Kent
61c   Dr. Julius Weber
62   George Whiteley/Photo Researchers, Inc.
63a   John M. Burnley/Photo Researchers, Inc.
63b   Joyce Photographics/Photo Researchers, Inc.
63c   Biophoto Associates/Photo Researchers, Inc.
64   E.R. Degginger/Photo Researchers, Inc.
65a   Thomas R. Taylor/Photo Researchers, Inc.
65b   Wolfgang Vogt

65c   Charles D. Winters
66   Louise K. Broman/Photo Researchers, Inc.
67a   Biophoto Associates/Photo Researchers, Inc.
67b   George Whiteley/Photo Researchers, Inc.
68   Jim Steinberg/Photo Researchers, Inc.
69a   E.R. Degginger/Photo Researchers, Inc.
69b   J. Beckett, M. Carruthers*
70   Andrew J. Martinez
71a   E.R. Degginger/Photo Researchers, Inc.
71b   Charles D. Winters
72   Ben Johnson/SPL/Photo Researchers, Inc.
73a   David Parker/SPL/Photo Researchers, Inc.
73b   George Whiteley/Photo Researchers, Inc.
74   Louise K. Broman/Photo Researchers, Inc.
75a   Gary Retherford/Photo Researchers, Inc.
75b   Joyce Photographics/Photo Researchers, Inc.
75c   Andrew J. Martinez
76   George Whiteley/Photo Researchers, Inc.
77a   Farrell Grehan/Photo Researchers, Inc.
77b   Charles R. Belinky/Photo Researchers, Inc.
78   Biophoto Associates/Photo Researchers, Inc.
79a   J. Beckett, M. Carruthers*
79b   Gary Retherford/Photo Researchers, Inc.
80   A.J. Copley/Visuals Unlimited
81a   Vaughan Fleming/SPL/Photo Researchers, Inc.
81b   A.J. Copley/Visuals Unlimited
82   Biophoto Associates/Photo Researchers, Inc.
83a   Joyce Photographics/Photo Researchers, Inc.
83b   Biophoto Associates/Photo Researchers, Inc.
84   George Whiteley/Photo Researchers, Inc.
85a   Wolfgang Vogt
85b   E.R. Degginger/Photo Researchers, Inc.
85c   Joyce Photographics/Photo Researchers, Inc.
86   E.R. Degginger/Photo Researchers, Inc.
87a   Tom McHugh/Photo Researchers, Inc.
87b   Thomas R. Taylor/Photo Researchers, Inc.
88   Wolfgang Vogt
89a   Vaughan Fleming/SPL/Photo Researchers, Inc.
89b   Breck P. Kent
90   Lincoln Nutting/Photo Researchers, Inc.
91a   Joyce Photographics/Photo Researchers, Inc.
91b   George Whiteley/Photo Researchers, Inc.
92   Charles D. Winters/Photo Researchers, Inc.
93a   E.R. Degginger/Color-Pic, Inc.
93b   Breck P. Kent
93c   Dr. Julius Weber
94   Margaret W. Carruthers
95a   James H. Robinson/Photo Researchers, Inc.
95b   A.J. Copley/Visuals Unlimited
96   George Whiteley/Photo Researchers, Inc.
97a   Ray Simons/Photo Researchers, Inc.
97b   George Whiteley/Photo Researchers, Inc.
98   M. Claye/Jacana/Photo Researchers, Inc.
99a   E.R. Degginger/Photo Researchers, Inc.
99b   Biophoto Associates/Photo Researchers, Inc.
100   Wolfgang Vogt

101a M. Claye/Jacana/Photo Researchers, Inc.
101b Ray Simons/Photo Researchers, Inc.
101c Biophoto Associates/Photo Researchers, Inc.
102 E.R. Degginger/Photo Researchers, Inc.
103a Biophoto Associates/Photo Researchers, Inc.
103b Tom McHugh/Photo Researchers, Inc.
103c Roberto de Gugliemo/SPL/Photo Researchers, Inc.
104 Andrew J. Martinez
105a Breck P. Kent
105b Breck P. Kent
105c Breck P. Kent
106 Breck P. Kent
107a Dr. Julius Weber
107b Joyce Photographics/Photo Researchers, Inc.
108 B. Walsh, J. Beckett, M. Carruthers*
109a B. Walsh, J. Beckett, M. Carruthers*
109b B. Walsh, J. Beckett, M. Carruthers*
110 B. Walsh, J. Beckett, M. Carruthers*
111a B. Walsh, J. Beckett, M. Carruthers*
111b Margaret W. Carruthers
112 Andrew J. Martinez
113a B. Walsh, J. Beckett, M. Carruthers*
113b B. Walsh, J. Beckett, M. Carruthers*
114 B. Walsh, J. Beckett, M. Carruthers*
115a Breck P. Kent
115b B. Walsh, J. Beckett, M. Carruthers*
116 Scott Camazine & Sue Trainor/Photo Researchers, Inc.
117a B. Walsh, J. Beckett, M. Carruthers*
117b Gregory G. Dimijian/Photo Researchers, Inc.
117c G. Carlton Ray/Photo Researchers, Inc.
118 John R. Foster
119a Andrew J. Martinez
119b Joyce Photographics/Photo Researchers, Inc.
119c Krafft/Explorer/Photo Researchers, Inc.
120 Ken M. Johns/Photo Researchers, Inc.
121a Ken M. Johns/Photo Researchers, Inc.
121b Richard Ash
121c Michael P. Gadomski/Photo Researchers, Inc.
122 Andrew J. Martinez
123a Breck P. Kent
123b Breck P. Kent
124 E.R. Degginger/Color-Pic, Inc.
125a Margaret W. Carruthers
125a Breck P. Kent
126 John Buitenkant/Photo Researchers, Inc.
127a Scott Camazine/Photo Researchers, Inc.
127b Kent Wood/Photo Researchers, Inc.
127c E.R. Degginger/Photo Researchers, Inc.

128 Ken M. Johns/Photo Researchers, Inc.
129a Breck P. Kent
129b B. Walsh, J. Beckett, M. Carruthers*
129c A.J. Copley/Visuals Unlimited
130 Ray Ellis/Photo Researchers, Inc.
131a Breck P. Kent
131b Breck P. Kent
131c Breck P. Kent
132 Andrew J. Martinez
133a B. Walsh, J. Beckett, M. Carruthers*
133b Joyce Photographics/Photo Researchers, Inc.
134 B. Walsh, J. Beckett, M. Carruthers*
135a B. Walsh, J. Beckett, M. Carruthers*
135b Ken Lucas/Visuals Unlimited
135c Courtesy of W.B. Hamilton/USGS
136 Breck P. Kent
137a George Bernard/SPL/Photo Researchers, Inc.
137b E.R. Degginger/Photo Researchers, Inc.
137c Tom McHugh/Photo Researchers, Inc.
138 B. Walsh, J. Beckett, M. Carruthers*
139a B. Walsh, J. Beckett, M. Carruthers*
139b Joyce Photographics/Photo Researchers, Inc.
140 E.R. Degginger/Color-Pic, Inc.
141a Breck P. Kent
141b Breck P. Kent
142 Breck P. Kent
143a John Foster/Photo Researchers, Inc.
143b Breck P. Kent
143c Ray Simons/Photo Researchers, Inc.
144a Vaughan Fleming/SPL/Photo Researchers, Inc.
144b Joyce Photographics/Photo Researchers, Inc.
145 François Gohier/Photo Researchers, Inc.
146a E.R. Degginger/Color-Pic, Inc.
146b Michael P. Gadomski/Photo Researchers, Inc.
147a B. Walsh, J. Beckett, M. Carruthers*
147b Ken Lucas/Visuals Unlimited
148 Ken Lucas/Visuals Unlimited
149a Charlie Ott/Photo Researchers, Inc.
149b E.R. Degginger/Photo Researchers, Inc.
152 Andrew J. Martinez
153 Charles D. Winters
154 Mark C. Burnett/Photo Researchers, Inc.
155 Biophoto Associates/Photo Researchers, Inc.
156 Phil Degginger/Color-Pic, Inc.

Front Cover: (*pyrite*) Mark C. Burnett/Photo Researchers, Inc.; (*sky*) Rafael Macia/Photo Researchers, Inc.

* Samples courtesy of American Museum of Natural History, New York.

Prepared and produced by
Chanticleer Press, Inc., and Chic Simple Design

Founder, Chanticleer Press, Inc.: Paul Steiner

Publisher, Chanticleer Press, Inc.: Andrew Stewart
Publishers, Chic Simple Design: Jeff Stone, Kim Johnson Gross

Chanticleer Staff:
Editor-in-Chief: Amy K. Hughes
Director of Production: Alicia Mills
Photo Editor: Zan Carter
Production Associate: Philip Pfeifer
Senior Editor: Lauren Weidenman
Managing Editors: Kristina Lucenko and Edie Locke
Editorial Assistant: Karin Murphy
Design Consultant: Marijka Kostiw
Design Intern: Anthony Liptak

Project Editors: Edward S. Barnard, Sharon Fass Yates
Bookmark Associates, Inc.

Chic Simple Design Staff:
Art Direction/Design: Takuyo Takahashi
Production/Design: Jinger Peissig
Project Coordinator: Gillian Oppenheim
Production: Camilla Marstrand
Design Interns: Kathryn Hammill, Danielle Huthart,
Diane Shaw, Sylvie Pusztaszeri

Writer (The world of rocks and minerals, How to look at rocks and minerals): Edward Ricciuti
Writer (Field Guide)/Consultant: Margaret W. Carruthers
Contributing Consultants: Carolyn R. Rebbert, Richard D. Ash
Copy Editor: Sarah Burns
Icon Illustrator: Holly Kowitt
Studio Photographer: David Bashaw

Scholastic Inc. Staff:
Editorial Director: Wendy Barish, Creative Director: David Saylor,
Managing Editor: Manuela Soares, Production Editor: Sean Gallagher,
Manufacturing Manager: Janet Castiglione

Original Series Design: Chic Simple Design, Takuyo Takahashi